# The Blood Runs Like a River Through My Dreams

Houghton Mifflin Company · Boston · New York

# The Blood
# Runs Like a River
# Through My Dreams

A  M E M O I R

*Nasdijj*

Visit our Web site: www.houghtonmifflinbooks.com

*Library of Congress Cataloging-in-Publication Data*

Nasdijj.
The blood runs like a river through my dreams : a memoir / Nasdijj.
p.   cm.
ISBN 0-618-04892-8
1. Nasdijj.   2. Navajo Indians—Biography.   3. Indians of North
America—Mixed descent.   4. Navajo Indians—Social life and customs.
5. Navajo Indian Reservation—Social conditions.   I. Title.

E99.N3 N26 2000
979.1004'972—dc21     00-038916

Book design by Anne Chalmers
Text type: Baskerville Monotype

Printed in the United States of America

QUM 10 9 8 7 6 5 4 3 2

Chapter 10 first appeared in *Esquire*.

AUTHOR'S NOTE

This work is a memoir and represents, to the best of my ability and my memory, an
accurate reporting of facts and events as I know them and as they have been told to
me. I have attempted to protect the privacy of people through the editorial decision to
frequently change names, appearances, and locations, as these are not relevant to the
focus of the work or the issues the work strives to deal with.

# CONTENTS

*The Blood Runs Like a River Through My Dreams*

# 1

# I Hate
# Mary Potato

*T*HE BACK OF my battered pickup truck is a mess. It is not unlike my life. My tools are always shifting around back there. Making clunking noises when the truck moves. I bought a camper shell so I could camp out in the back of my truck. Now groceries don't blow away on my way home from the grocery store.

I bought a new hydraulic jack. There's my fishing stuff back

there. Poles. A net. There's an old pair of cowboy boots I don't
wear because I wore them out. Some things are harder to
throw away than other things. Those cowboy boots walked
through a lot of memories. There's a hundred-pound bag of
dog food I was supposed to drop off at the Wolf Ranch in
Ramah for the wolves but I keep forgetting about it. There's a
cement block I use as a weight to get me through snow. There
are my tire chains I never use, as putting on tire chains in the
Big Mud (the Navajo term for the terrain in this part of New
Mexico) is about as much fun as wrestling with an ornery pig.
And there's a basketball that rolls around back there every time
I turn a corner.

Mary Potato bought the basketball. "Boys play basketball,"
she said. The basketball was a birthday gift for Tommy. Tommy
Nothing Fancy was my Navajo son. Tommy Nothing Fancy is
dead.

He was a little brown guy with lungs. When Tommy was an
infant, he'd cry louder than a coyote wails against the moon. I
can still hold both his cowboy boots with one hand.

Jet-black hair. Almost blue. Eyes the soft color of the Navajo
mountains. Tommy was beautiful. In his own way, the boy was
perfect, even if perfection is relative. My Indian wife and I took
Tom into our hearts and into our home when he was brand
spanking new. The particulars are irrelevant. Infants are like
freight trains. We did not know Tommy had fetal alcohol syndrome. I do not know if it would have mattered had we known
about the FAS ahead of time. How can anyone be ahead of
time for anything? We were not ready for FAS but there it was.
You deal with it or you don't.

Seizures mainly. And an otherness about the eyes. They
would cross when he was mad, which was regular.

But the kid had spunk. Tom loved to fish and he loved to play basketball, although he never learned to dribble very well. He would use both his hands. And Tommy loved riding around Navajoland in Old Big Wanda, my Ford F150 with the camper shell. Even as an infant, Tommy would be hypnotized by the velocity of the truck along the reservation roads and the red rock horizons of the Navajo.

I call that truck a reservation truck because it has pits and bashes yet it runs well. It has survived Big Mud, Big Winter, and the big old loads of piñon wood. Whenever I clean Old Big Wanda I always find new pockets of reservation mud caked to her. That pickup is of the earth. She's the kind of truck migrant workers drive, sometimes live in. A mongrel migrant vehicle, and it is owned by a mongrel migrant.

My parents were migrant workers, and my cowboy daddy had trucks just like Old Big Wanda. We worked the ranches of the West and crops anywhere. My cowboy dad was white. My mother's people were with the Navajo.

Mary Potato was a Navajo, too. She looked like a Navajo. I never did ask to see her papers. Why would I? It was none of my business. Mary Potato could say she was anything. She could have been a Kickapoo for all I knew. I did not care one way or the other what tribe she was from. If she wanted to claim she was a Navajo, then let her. Most folks in Gallup are all Navajo or part Navajo or they live among the Navajo because the Navajo are the majority and not the minority in this place. I did my best to ignore Mary Potato. My policy was to ignore drunks who wanted money. Usually they'd go away, but ignoring Mary Potato did not always work. "You're white," she said to me one day in the city park.

That and fifty cents gets you on the bus.

"My folks were migrant workers, and we worked ranches all around here," I tried to explain. I loathe explaining it. White folks particularly always have to know the exact spot you are from. I'm from everywhere. For the life of me I cannot see why it matters.

Most migrants are Hispanic. But not this time.

Mary Potato claimed she knew what it was like to work in fields. This did not surprise me in the least, as I had known many, many Indians who had lived something of the migrant life. I knew Chippewa who picked cherries. I knew Muckleshoot Indians who picked apples. I knew Ute Indians who baled hay during baling season. I knew Red Lake Band Chippewa who worked sugar beets. I knew Alabama-Coushatta who picked Texas cotton. I knew Cherokee who worked tobacco. I knew Fort Sill Apaches who worked melons. I knew Seminoles who picked tomatoes. The Navajo work with sheep. Sometimes horses. Sometimes cows. But the fields I knew Mary Potato worked were mainly plowed in bars and saloons in Gallup, New Mexico, watering holes of gin and sin. I did not care where she was from. It was irrelevant. She knew a hardness. She knew loss.

Mary Potato gave Tommy the basketball. She knew he would love it.

The Navajo boys love basketball. Reservation basketball.

There was an old rusted basketball hoop attached precariously with screws to a telephone pole not far from where I lived on the Navajo Nation, and Navajo boys would come here to play basketball on the blacktop where the asphalt met the dirt road and the reservation mud. Big snow deterred them but ice on the asphalt did not deter them.

It was pretty basic basketball. No frills. No coaches. No net. Someone had stolen the net years ago. The lone, rusted rim was in perpetual danger of falling off the telephone pole every time a basketball made deadly contact. But Navajo boys would come here and play informal pickup games.

The little boys particularly liked coming, though they could never commandeer what passed for a basketball court for very long, as the older boys would show up, start their games, and elbow the little guys like Tommy out of the way.

But Tommy had something not all of the little Navajo boys had. Tommy had a new basketball. He wasn't much bigger than the ball itself, and the older boys—older being maybe twelve—would tolerate his presence if Tom showed up with his ball.

The game begins. In time, the suave patience of the bigger boys with the little pretzels would grow thin, strained, and eventually it would wear out: Tommy would sit there sniffling on the sidelines, content (or forced) to watch the Navajo boys with their long flowing hair show off their adolescent stuff. Pose and strut. Pumped up. Free throws. Take the shot. Little boys wanting to be big boys and big boys wanting to be men. Fetal alcohol syndrome or no fetal alcohol syndrome, the boys always want to be men. I knew better than to interfere. Any father wants his son to learn how to defend himself some.

When Tommy was diagnosed with fetal alcohol syndrome my wife wept for a week.

There was little help to be had for it.

So I did exactly what I think all parents should not do: I spoiled him rotten. I wasn't rich, but I could give him certain things. I could try to teach the boy to dribble, and I could teach the boy to fish. More than anything, I was determined to do this for Tommy. I would not allow fetal alcohol syndrome or whatever to ruin that for me, or for him, and I did teach him to fish, and gently.

Fishing is a gentle business when you're out on a lake or in a Rocky Mountain stream. Fishing is a gentle business anywhere on the Navajo Nation. Ramah Lake. Blue Water Lake. If Tommy had been confined to a wheelchair (which he was not), I would have pushed that chair into any number of rivers. The San Juan River, where there was a private spot of sand where we could fish and swim, was Tommy's favorite place. We went there often.

I was damn well determined that Tom would not have the kind of grinding migrant life I'd had. No matter how many years I might or might not have with him. Ask anyone who has lost a kid. All we ever have is now. He would not be knocked around relentlessly like I had been knocked around all my life. I would do it differently.

Tommy was the one thing I did that was good and didn't fail. The rest of it is ephemeral. The fetal alcohol syndrome was a reality. I gave him happiness and joy and fishing tackle and trucks and dogs. I would do it again.

"I didn't mean to have him," Mary Potato said.

Tom and I were playing in a park in town. Swings. Sandbox. Teeter-totter. Monkey bars.

At first, I had thought she was just another town drunk. People were always coming up and talking to us and engaging us in conversation if they could. People needed booze and change. I had neither. I had seen Mary Potato around like you see people around, but I had never directly engaged her, as I am apt to avoid such people. In fact, I avoid people whenever I can, which is never enough.

"I had a boy who would be his age but they took him from me," Mary Potato said.

Why I attract the losers from everywhere in the universe I do not know. Like a magnet. She's watching Tommy with a glaze that is mainly sadness. I know that look. It's about what you do not have.

Mary Potato claimed she was Tommy's natural mom. I was doubtful. I was angry. I was angry this strange woman approached us. I was angry she was making some kind of claim to what was mine.

"I don't want him back," she said.

Good. She wasn't getting him back. Over my dead body.

"I just wanted you to know about me." She paused. "That I'm there."

I was angry she had to be a drunk. I was angry she had done this to this kid — and if not this kid, some other kid with FAS. Some other kid who had seizures and who would never read goddamn English. Some other kid whose teachers would say *try harder!* and who climbed the walls. Some other kid who never slept. Some other kid in some other family.

I was angry she would even attempt to speak with me. (It took me years to realize how carefully she actually did it, making sure Tommy was far enough away so as to be kept out of it, and I thank her for that.) I was angry her life was like a wound. I was angry she had had her children taken away. I was angry she was a hooker. I was angry all the medicine men in the world could not cure her life to balance. I did not want to know that she was there.

*That I'm there,* she said.

It was too much to ask of me.

But there she was, her body hunched over the picnic table. She could have been my Tommy's mom. It was possible even if

I didn't think it was probable. She could have been *my* mom. She was like my mom. My mother was a hopeless drunk. I would use the word "alcoholic," but it's too polite. It's a white people word. Alcoholic. In the migrant life, what we knew was falling-down Jezus drunk and puked again. There's nothing polite about cleaning up your mother in her vomit and dragging her unconscious carcass back to the migrant housing trailer you lived in. Daddy, too. The story is ordinary. Mama usually just passed out wherever she happened to be. I'd find her in the back of pickups all the time. With men. For all of Mary Potato's failures, they did not match the failures of my mom. And I loved my mom. Even if I was (and am) angry with her.

Mary Potato was a whore who had been kicked off the reservation and lived in a shack made of toothpicks and tarpaper and magazines out by the railroad tracks. Mama had it worse. My dad would sell my mom to other migrant men for five bucks. The life Mary Potato lived was a walk in the park and a ride on the teeter-totter compared to the life my mother lived. Mary Potato could have been my mom. In another life. I could have been Mary Potato. Easily. How can another human being measure what she has given up?

How do you divorce loss from rage? If I let the rage out, it will destroy everything. Wolves! I do not let it out, do not tell this story lightly. I cannot speak of it aloud. Or only to people who are close to me, and even then I try hard to leave out the darker pieces of it.

"I didn't mean to have him, but these things happen," Mary Potato said.

I'm minding my own business at the picnic table. Tommy is off on his squeaky swing. Me in my brooding silence. As is my way.

I had known Mary Potato in other incarnations. On other reservations. She did not want him back.

"I just wanted you to know," she repeated, "that I'm there."

*That I'm there.* A recognition of obscurity and existence.

Somewhere around the late 1940s, my mom and my dad met in a bar in Gallup. I think they died somewhere in one, too. Bit by bit. In fragments. In tequila shots. In some vast midnight whiskey mist my parents seemed to simply slip away. They did not have far to go. We existed at the edges: the edges of the migrant camps, the edges of the Rio Grande, the edges of the horse-poor ranches we lived on, the edges of the reservation.

The Navajo Nation.

The Taos Pueblo.

The Acoma Indian Reservation.

The Jicarilla Apache Reservation.

The Ramah Navajo.

The Mescalero Apache Indian Reservation.

The Ute Indian Reservation.

Anywhere there were ranches and cows to work, or sheep to shear, or crops to pick or harvest.

Texas cotton. Colorado wheat.

New Mexico roundups. Castrating calves and stompin' feet.

I have seen my share of the insides of those Gallup bars. Even as a kid, my dad, the cowboy, brought me to enough of them. Those strong Indian men laughing and putting me up on the pool table where I could spin around like entertainment. Pulling my dad out of those Gallup bars in the 1950s, always fights among the men, the women quite content to step over my daddy's stinking piece of breathing meat. Me getting that man back to his cowboy truck. I could have used those strong pool-table arms then. Gallup or El Paso, it was all the same to me, as it would be the same to any kid.

I never put my son through that wringer.

The first memory I have is of a time my mother and I were under a tree. I do not know where. I think the desert. I am sitting naked in a big white ceramic pan, and the pan is filled with cold water. I am having a ball. Just splashing water underneath a tree. There is a line of clothes hung out and drying in the desert heat. The air is very dry. My mother's hands dipping into the coolness of the water.

She leaves. She does not come back.

I'm still angry about the life Mary Potato is forced to live. I say "forced to live" because I know her options are so limited as to be almost nonexistent. Truckers could turn off I-40, make a quick trek down old Route 66—U-Haul Central, the Wild West Shangri-La Road Motel parking lot, Palm Tree Trinket Shop and Indian Curios, Uranium Mine Museum, Pizza Hut, feed store, Tortilla Emporium, drive-up liquor store, Powwow Park—and pull their rigs into the lot. Strangers popping Mary in the motel dark. Mary got slammed around. Black eyes, broken bones. She was brittle.

Mary Potato's children had been taken from her. Other people raise them now.

I live with fetal alcohol syndrome, too. I saw my mother go through whole bottles of vodka while she was pregnant, and she was a heavy drinker when she had me. I saw her lose babies. At least they were lucky enough not to be born alive.

It is very unusual that someone with this disease would become a writer. But I am stubborn and perverse. I am also more than a little angry, which is probably why I was so damn determined I would do good by Tom. Tommy was my sweet revenge. That he could experience joy and all the good things that make life worth living was my salvation. Now he is gone. Writing is my new revenge. That I can put any of it down in the limited confines of the English language is a salvation of sorts.

I would rather have my Tom than this writing about him, which is just about all I have now. Sweating blood over words is anything but simple, and English is a foreign language I do not readily understand. I became a writer to piss on all the many white teachers and white editors out there (everywhere) who insisted it could not be done. Not by the stupid mongrel likes of me. Tom was like me and had little respect for authority. You had to earn it. I did.

These expert people in the vast universe of writing were not too different from the people who always told me Tommy Nothing Fancy was hopeless. Fetal alcohol syndrome is a mean buzzard. Tommy was many things, but hopeless was not one of them. I understood his battles with the things he saw, like words on the printed page. Reading is a real struggle. It's extremely hard work. Things appear upside down. Writing is worse. My new babies are the stories I tell as I have lived them, touched them, been touched by them, lived through them, and survived them. They are my feeble attempt to bring the dead to life. I will paint a picture of my Tommy here.

In order to succeed as a writer, you have to grow some pretty thick, scarred skin, and you have to get used to lots and lots of failure. FAS actually prepares you pretty well. Failure is the landscape and the barriers. I am not glad to have FAS. I am not glad Tom had it. FAS killed him. It is hard for me to be compassionate toward whatever human being or set of circumstances gave him this horrible thing. Try as I might, I cannot bring him back. Sometimes kids with FAS have very serious seizures. The medications Tommy took stopped working. It happened gradually. The seizures got worse. No one knows why.

I still have the rivers and the horses and the mountains and the mesas and the red rocks soft with sand. And a basketball I keep in the back of my pickup truck. That basketball rolls around back there with my other junk like the past that will give me no peace. Someday I am going to find some deserving six-year-old to give it to.

Even if Mary Potato was Tom's natural mom, she wasn't there. Mary Potato wasn't there when my Tom was sick. She wasn't there when he was having seizures. She wasn't there to make bunny patches for his knees. She wasn't there when all you're left with is the phone in the middle of the night. I was there in the middle of the night. I was there through the seizures. I was there in hospitals in White People Town with medical specialists who knew nothing. I was there when they said he would never learn anything. I was there when I proved them wrong.

We did not see Mary Potato often. But I knew now she was out there. In the dark with the wolves. Like a shadow.

She called. I was not amused. I do not know how she managed to get my number. It was his birthday—she claimed—and she was coming over with a basketball she had purchased as a birthday gift.

I hung up the phone. She knew where we lived. It was not his birthday. She arrived in an ancient Buick filled with men.

I would not let her in. But I would take the basketball if she agreed to leave. I took the basketball. The muffler dangling from the Buick like a broken limb dragging, limping, scraping blue-hot dragon's breath all along the asphalt as they left my place for the dragon bars in Gallup. Back to the good life, or in any case the life they knew.

My dog and I drive to Mary Potato's sad place. Navajo hogans can be poor, but none of them are as poor as the bare-bones tarpaper shacks folks live in at the edges of White People Town. I did not let Mary come to Tommy's funeral. Now, the least I owed her was a ride.

When you live on the reservation, you give rides to people who do not have transportation. That's just the way it is. That's all it was. A ride.

Mary Potato keeps a big black mongrel dog clipped to a chain on a cottonwood tree in the front yard. She is almost ready.

I sit on the couch and wait. The house smells of swamp tea and old underwear and boiled roots and dark rooms. Faded Jesus yellow on the wall. Gin. Years and years of cigarettes. Mary Potato walks slowly, with the knowledge she will never heal. How many knife blades have plunged into her solitary heart only to find their way into her belly where all her reversals and her hollow aching live. She does not dance on the wind with mad wings but is blown into her dreams of savage incapacity. There is no refuge in her house, which shakes like toothpicks with the passing of the train. What seems to live here is contempt. She is tough because she has to be.

Finally, she is ready. She wanted to look nice. She is dignified.

I have a hard time keeping the truck on the road. The closer I get to where Tommy is buried, the closer I come to knowing I know nothing. Everything I have ever known has been taken from me. My only grip is on the steering wheel. Everything at the periphery of my vision is compressed, and all I can see is what's directly in front of Old Big Wanda. I know Mary Potato has been talking. About her life. Who can estimate what she has given up? I am no judge of anything. I am no moral judge of Mary Potato. I am only a man giving a woman a ride to a cemetery. Go, go, and the wind just sings.

He needs me. He is cold. I cannot be here long. I fall apart.

This woman who says she gave birth to my son smokes a cigarette and walks around looking at the other graves. She takes a plastic rose from her purse and sticks it into the almost frozen ground. We do not say much. Certainly nothing meaningful. The Navajo abhor speaking of the dead.

We drive back to Mary Potato's place in White People Town. Junkyards. Rusted vehicles piled high as a mountain. It is getting late. I do not go inside. We talk a little in the truck. She is soft and sad. It is difficult to hate her or keep my anger burning like it was some nuclear vehemence. I will never have to see her again. She still thinks Tommy was her son, and I still doubt it. It doesn't matter what I think. What matters is we both have lost fragments of ourselves to wolves of adversity. Life.

I leave her and start to drive home. The weather shifts and it begins to snow. The New Mexico sky deepens, casting purple shadows along the roadside ditch. The night comes down. The close dark. Something out there howling. Rocky Mountain snow sharp as ice picks. The old Navajo songs in my grandmother's mouth. The snow coming down harder than a bar fight. Old Big Wanda slips on a crusty patch of ice. We slide slow motion down into an arroyo. The dog and I are stuck and will need someone to pull us out of here. No one comes along. We will be here until morning. Navajo folks in their trucks will arrive eventually. Someone will have a chain. Someone will help pull the fool out of the snow.

Only thing to do is crawl into the back of the vehicle, into the sleeping bag with the dog, and stay as warm as possible. Avoid frostbite if I can. A numbness. It is impossible to sleep.

I turn over on my side and come face to face with the basketball. He always dribbled it with two hands. Never one. I put the basketball underneath my shirt so I might see what it looks and feels like to be pregnant. It is not the same. The basketball is light and empty. Tommy Nothing Fancy was never empty. His quarrels with the world were never light. They were grave battles, and he met them head on with the hardiness of who he was.

In the old days, the Navajo disposed of their dead in the branches of trees, where the spirit lingers. Tom's burial is still crushing me, and time does not make it better. The basketball still rolls around in my pickup. I cannot rid myself of it, or of Mary Potato. And the wind sings go, go. The ghostly laughing voices of the Navajo.

# 2

# My Son
# Comes Back to Me

*M*Y SON comes back to me when I least expect to see his ghostly vision. Often I am able to see him clearly when I close my eyes. Sometimes when I see him he's still a little guy. Other times he's older, as he would be now, and I am likely to see him in a group of rowdy children. Children riding on buses. Children playing on playgrounds. Children who have been dismissed from school. Children running like runaway horses. Go, go.

My son comes back to me sometimes as I'm cooking, and, not thinking, I unconsciously cook enough for the two of us. My son comes back to me when I am alone on the porch and watching the stars. He's in the shadows and the sounds, more thought than reality, barely visible, his obsidian eyes gleaming with a supple and eternal fire. My son comes back to me in ordinary places like barbershops, where little boys have to sit and be still, something Tommy Nothing Fancy found very hard to do, and so I cut his hair myself once, making a real mess of it. My son comes back to me when I forget about things like time and dust. I often see him when I'm fishing. He's on the shore of the river just down from me a ways. Or he's fishing from a rock. My son comes back to me when the light spills down the canyon's walls and howls at the moving vanity of the river.

There had always been a simmering rebellion in who he was. He had a quick, impetuous mind, and he could be impulsive. A pony.

My son comes back to me whenever I find myself driving across the great expanse that is America. I have driven across the country at least twenty times. In search of what, I cannot really know. I go, go with the singing of the wind. Tommy Nothing Fancy sits beside the dog, who rests her head against his knee. I tell myself that the reason I drive to so many remote and lonely places is to check out the fishing. I won't fish just anywhere. There has to be some kind of allure to it. A remoteness that says the fishing here could be the best fishing anywhere. Places not yet ruined by people. I have to like the name of a place.

Portage. Geraldine. Blackfoot. Walla Walla. Bighorn. Custer. Ten Sleep. Canyon Creek. And the wind sings go, go.

My son comes back to me in the singing of the wind. In the

singing of the fish line as I cast for trout. He's just over there beyond the bend. I have never accepted his death.

Whenever I want to see him, all I have to do is put the dog in the truck and go.

Go.

Fort Peck Lake. The Shoshone River. Thunderbird Mesa. House-of-Hands Cave. Elephant Butte. Chaco Canyon. Lukachukai. Yellow Horse Ruins. Ramah Lake.

I think I know the way.

"We're lost again," he says.

I do not always respond to the lucid observations of ghosts.

My son comes back to me at night, when sleep circles its heathen wings all around you and is about to take you up. He lives in my bones and my scars. My son comes back to me and this time I do not nag him about washing his hands with soap, eating his vegetables, picking up his socks, the toys in his room. There is a fierceness to him now that seems to crackle through his veins, our old skirmishes forgotten. We are travelers together through this blossoming dankness. I wonder if he has a suitcase. He smiles and turns away.

My son comes back to me whenever I heal just a little, and he approves of my deliverance and announces that his own invisible flaws were merely fragments of my baffled imagination, and no one — not he, not I — believes this. My son comes back to me as the future floats along like the passing of the landscape in a soundless vehicle. Destitute, I force a smile in return, even as I fall away.

"Tell me about these fireflies," he says. And so I do, although I cannot think to find my wisdom concerning butterflies and other creatures. My son comes back to me with his enormous weight upon my chest, and I fly out of my being here to somewhere else where the sun floods my aching with a voice like broken glass. His captivity an entombment where I rebirth his architecture again and again.

"How long will it take for us to get there?" he wants to know.

I glance over at him in the truck. Only knowing that we're on our way to somewhere. Someplace where the answers of the fathers to the questions of the sons resonate with reason.

He never arrives with a suitcase, which means he cannot stay. My own unclaimed baggage is the world. When he comes into my room at night I ask, "Are you thirsty?"

He nods.

I stand in front of the white enamel bathroom sink and drink a foreign bitterness. I am not a bitter man. Just forsaken some. I cast off this choking knot around my throat that constricts the waking moments. You realize aloneness is a collection of small accessible things passing by you down a glistening anonymous corridor. Go, go. Outside are the undaunted bursts of rhythm from the road we traveled as though it were delirium. He is standing in his pajamas by my bed. Thirsty and transformed, staring at nothing, refusing to listen to my poor excuse for reason. I ramble along these roads alone, the oncoming lights of grinding trucks stretching like distant solitary stars that illuminate their grip in space.

My son comes back to me in exile, removed from the tumultuous world of children, removed from the silent world of men. Whoever you are holding my hand, our mutual demise speaks tongues of solitude we cannot escape. I still have a collection of your crayon drawings—horses, dogs, jet planes, wars, cars—brief moments of your passage here, caricatures of reprieve and stick men's splendor. My son comes back to me whispering the small intrigues of ordinary memories, my teaching him how to tie his shoes when I can barely tie my own.

My son comes back to me in radiance on nights the wind sings treacherous awakenings and the moon seems but a paralytic rock suspended in a regal sky of blackened teeth. The essence of my existence has been changed by his mysterious appearances. "Are you thirsty? Go back to bed." His vision disappears with the coming of the morning sun, and I know I have invented him again as I scale these cliffs of disbelief whose gravity and dimensions crumble at the slightest introspection.

We take our vehicle onto the mesa, a flat, unbroken place where he sits on my lap and drives for the distance of a city block — no road here to have to follow — bouncing over prairie dogs' holes, me working gas and brakes, him laughing, flourishes in his giggling irrepressibility, adrenaline giving both of us a particular sustenance, my leg going numb. My son comes back to me from distant realms unburdened by reality like a lullaby. He's been crying in his crib, he must be thirsty, and no amount of rocking brings him comfort. No somnolent whispers here. I put him in the vehicle for a long humming ride through the urgent night.

Tommy was always spectacular.

3

# Runaway Horses

*T*HE BOY looks forward. The man looks back. The two only rarely merge. But when they do there is a dialogue with the present.

As an adult, I used to live next door to an Indian school on the Navajo Nation. The Navajo Nation, the largest of all the Indian reservations, sits like an island in the middle of a rolling, arid desert. A desert alive with things. My favorite morning thing to do was to sit on my back porch, drinking coffee from a hot tin cup, and watch the Navajo children noisily arrive on the bus for another day of whatever goes on in a school composed of Navajo children.

Some children walked. The children who walked to school often had dogs who followed them all the way to the school building, and then the dogs would spend the rest of the day waiting for their charges to walk home again. It was a place of kids and dogs and horses and sheep and goats and cows and coyotes.

There was a baseball field, too. The kids played there. The dogs romped there. The horses and the cattle ate the grass on the baseball field. The old woman who lived down the dirt road from me let her goats and her sheep eat the grass in the baseball field as well. I only rarely went inside the school. I was asked once to be a judge at the school's science fair. I went to country-western dances in the cafeteria, held at night while various Navajo would covertly drink beer in the parking lot. Even at night you could feel the presence of eyes watching you. The eyes belonged to a wild horse who lived there.

At the school.

No one knew where he came from.

Perhaps he came from a herd of runaway horses.

I have been homeless like a runaway horse.

Whenever I left my house at night, I could hear the wild horse breathing in the shadows.

You could smell him, too. The smell was a mix of rotten old rope and barn. Not that this horse had ever been in a barn. This horse was definitely not civilized. He had never known the restraint of a rope.

Sometimes I would feel movement, look up, and he'd be

there, staring through a window at us creatures who lived in-
doors. The horse was insanely curious. Most wild horses are
more skittish than curious. This horse was different. There
were Navajo who saw the wild stallion as something of a spirit.
He was that, and other things.

Strip the romance away and you've got an uppity horse stuck
solid with dirt and burrs. Stinks like a squished skunk in the
middle of the road. The smell is awful something considerable.
The tail is a mass of knotted hair and weeds. Poor thing. No
one can catch it.

Many Navajo tried.

The stallion is nervous. He likes watching children. Now, this
is where I'm supposed to say that wild stallions can be dangerous. Wild stallions can be dangerous. Get too close and this one
bares his yellow teeth. He will bite you, too. There were several
meetings at the Mariano Lake chapter house about what to do
with the stallion situation. Not all the Navajo agreed. It was not
unusual to find that consensus here was elusive. White people
find a solidity among the Indians that only exists to prop up already established stereotypical expectations. There was no consensus as to what to do about the wild horse who lived at the
school down the dirt road. There were Navajo folks who maintained that a wild stallion at a school was not good. Someone
could get hurt. We never knew exactly who this someone might
be, but whoever he was, he called Animal Control in Crownpoint. Animal Control came with tranquilizer guns, but they
never got close to hitting the stallion. Finally they gave up, and
the stallion just sort of blended into the landscape because he
was always there, a fixture in the background like the soft
brown rise of Hosta Butte.

The stallion never did grasp the concept of limits. He never understood that he was trespassing. He never absorbed any of the boundaries.

He had to be a runaway.

When no one was around I fed him oats. He was always hoongry. Yet he made it very clear that if I moved too quickly he wouldn't hesitate to kick me. I have seen wild horses disembowel cowboys who walked behind them.

Walking behind a horse is a dangerous thing to do.

When it comes to horses, my romanticism is limited to what is and is not real. A wild animal has an innate ability to protect itself. Living in the wild is a tricky business. We are all survivors here.

He never attacked anyone.

He liked my neighbor's mares.

Cowboys came to catch him. The cowboys went home exhausted. It was not possible to catch this horse. You had to know that he had to come to you.

He never had a name. I toyed with names once, but assigning a name to this animal might be dangerous. You might own him then.

Sometimes whole herds of wild horses would sweep down from the mountains, chests heaving, bolting, tremors suddenly absorbed by the essence of the earth. A pilgrimage of horses, ecstasy, seeming to come from somewhere beneath the liquefied ground. An insurrection waged by runaway horses, bold, flown, a sorcery of vanished gates. Running perilously like an arterial bombardment. Whole herds of heart and horses thunder down abandoned fields at the tops of mesas marbled red by sandstone cliffs riddled with yellow veins of desert rock. No one seems to own these mad animals. Mad to run. Mad to carry themselves with a rancorous tenseness past ancient caves that rumble with the vibration of hooves. Mad to explode and just plain mad. There is a difference between the sane, broken horse you ride — acclimated to his saddle and his reins — and the mad animals who hauled themselves here. A primitive bearing-down.

Rolling clouds of desert dust barrel after them like snow cascades down a higher, blacker sovereignty. Bursting forth, rapturous, biting, fighting, mean, posturing, flying through the dark of demons rendered fixed in the face of storms of horses shot through with dread and terror. There is no solace in the eyes of runaway horses. No human hand to tame them with metal bits and leather straps. No loyalties allowing them to fathom the cattle guards and fences that hem them in. Bewildered, they are free to roam the landscape rather than submit. Whole herds of horses spooked by lightning running in alignment with the leaves along the hollow of an uneven cottonwood stream. Whole herds of running horses avoid that wide abyss where the smell of humans lingers in the lower depths and boys with ropes behind their backs slowly approach the skittish, dominant stallions. Herds of mad running animals fall back upon the circuit of the stars, and landscape's wreckage is a ribcage of surrender. No one knows where these horses come from and no one knows where they go when they disappear forever from the sun. Whole herds of runaways launched like the prow of a ship into the waves at sea, ripping up the paradox of the world that contains them.

One day I was driving my pickup, Old Big Wanda, with my dog in the front seat. I call my dog Navajo. The Navajo think it's funny I would name my dog after the tribe, but being part Indian (or so my mama claimed), part mongrel, always fragmented, I'm allowed to call my dog anything I want. We passed a dead horse in a ditch being chewed apart by coyotes.

The heads of the coyotes were stuck inside the bloody belly of the unfortunate creature. It was a noisy feeding frenzy, the kind of thing you might see on a National Geographic TV special. But this was not Africa. I sat in my truck and stared. Navajo passed by in their trucks, totally oblivious.

I have always thought of him somehow as *my* horse.

He had been hit by a vehicle, probably on the road at night. It was always a possibility. Drunks here are always hitting someone's sheep, but why you would let your sheep out onto the road was another question entirely. I was known as one of the take-care-of-your-livestock fanatics. It seemed only fair.

The coyotes were growling, and they didn't run like they normally do when a human being gets that close. This was a feast and they weren't about to be deprived of it. The coyotes yipped and tore off what was left of one of the massive legs. They ran with it, dragging it through the mud of the ditch, but the leg was too heavy and my presence finally unnerved them, and they dropped it.

I got out of the pickup and stood over what was left of the wild animal.

He had always loved eating grass in the baseball field.

In three days' time there was no evidence the wild stallion had ever existed. Nature gives. Nature watches. Nature evaporates and disappears. There is a relentless spirit to the beauty in nature. There is death, too. There is no waste in nature. Not a shred. Everything is food.

Even his big bones had been sacrificed.

Sometimes I drove to the spot where his body had been, at the side of the road that goes into White People Town, not far from the Pinedale Trading Post (where there are coin-operated washers and dryers). I could feel his spirit rising up through the ground.

Biting. Snorting. Kicking. Catch me if you can. No one ever could. I say some prayers to Sa, the Navajo deity of endurance and age. And death, which is why the Navajo only rarely speak of Sa directly. I do not know her well, but feel as if I have known her forever.

It is a hard thing to live freely in the wild. It is a thing of enormous, breathtaking contradiction. There is not a shred of romance to it. Not too far away, the sound of children playing baseball at a school. The crack of a bat. Cheering. The afternoon light slants down from a sky shot with the bare and unspeakable. The sky is a desert with the vast hot smell of dust. We are all runaway horses. We are all draped across the backs of horses, desperately hanging on. A phenomenon of ecstasy, a pilgrimage, an insurrection, and a carnage, recapitulated forever. A sorcery of gates now closed, and the horses—captured —dance round and round.

# 4

# Emergency
# Landing

WHEN MAMA told Indian stories you had to watch her eyes.
They could dance and sing in the telling of a story. When
Mama told Indian stories you also had to listen to the sym-
phony and watch the light show that went on behind the eyes.

Mama in her rooms candlelit with her illuminated folktales
and her whiskey glass. You could play with her shot glass. It was
heavy and could not be broken, but was chipped slightly at the
lip, which rendered it imperfect as a shot glass, glamorous in

the way good dice are glamorous. Perfect as a plaything, if you can call such adult objects and adult folktales with their violence playthings. Like Mama. She was called Shima.

Women themselves could be playthings. This is how we saw them because this is how they were treated by men who were absurd.

Whenever we moved into a new place we had to scrub it down to make it clean. Mama made it quite clear that I may have been born in a ditch but it didn't mean I had to act like I lived in one. Sometimes we didn't have cleaning soap—Mama liked the ones that smelled of pine—but just used water to wash everything down. "And get rid of someone else's dirt," she'd say.

It never mattered where we were or where we were going or where we had been. Time and place were not important. Mama told stories to keep her children entertained, but there was more to it than that. Mama was a storyteller because it was what she had to give. She would gather all the children around her and her hands would fly. But it was her eyes that drew you in. In to a place of deserts and mountains and rough terrain where animals could speak and the War Twins confronted great and powerful monsters. It didn't matter where we were. Mama could tell her stories on the road.

Buzzard country. Needles, California, from a Jeepster. Cactus. Las Vegas blacktop shimmering in the heat. The train station in Denver. Salt Lake City bus stop. Downtown Seattle. Bismarck, North Dakota. Alcatraz. Chinatown. Fishing off the coast of Santa Cruz. The Au Sable River in Michigan. Canoes. Trucks. The back seats of cars and scrunched again. Tampa. Key West. Boats. Indian towns in Canada. The South, which meant Mississippi. Bags of oranges. Boiled potatoes with salt. Fast food. Picnics. Detours. You ate what you were served. You did not complain. You accepted. Mother would wash us with a wet washcloth. Even in the midst of chaos you had to be clean. And if there was no water around she would give you a spit bath with spit on a Kleenex. Old tin tubs. You stood still while she did this. Messed with you. You did not wiggle. She did it on buses, trains, in cars. She washed her children in public places. The traveling life wasn't aimless and it wasn't wandering as long as there was a destination, and there was always a destination. Dots on a map.

Then back again.

Different routes. Different ranches. Different crops. Different animals.

If she gave you a spit bath you smelled like her for at least a week.

It was a life tossed about the waves, tossed about malcontented confrontation, tossed about a desert of wishes, tossed and tangled with the branches and the roots of other thrown-together lives. It was a life grinding its slow way through chaos, through hot places where nothing stirs, through the opposing needs of individuals where defeat is not so much a game you play but a path through wreckage, and where survival is a story your mother tells of beautiful things gone mad, and rapids, twisting, stirring, swimming in the constellations of the stories she creates like some great pain is forever freed and dances now along these roads of austere nerves where hunger sinks its teeth into the belly.

It was a life tossed about a labyrinth of fields, and rusted plows, and Lotaburger, too, across the street from the broken motel where we lived like flies above the sassafras. It was a life tossed about by the wrestling and the power of the dinosaurs we lived with, men usually, who, not knowing what else to do with us, would lift us up and set us laughing on their drunken shoulders, tough with the stolen armor of the enemy, relentless in their pursuit of all the things they wanted, and the way they wanted them, as if that were why the rest of us were here, to service their demands and their shortages and their boots and their laundry with our washing it clean again and again. It was a life where children came in packages, and beds were shared with cousins, and sleep was just another worthless yielding you pretended to do as the adults sat outside the motel room in metal garden chairs and argued, and drank, and played cards, and forbade the world to leave them behind, and gauged their weaknesses as if they were a house of judges in a hierarchy of listed pains, trawling with their nets the depths for random revelations, finding little there, pushing back that dogfish place where their luck fell in.

It was a life tossed about all the nice arrangements, where Daddy comes home from work to eat his dinner cooked by Mom with the family and the Tater Tots. His hands could pick you apart, your insect wings, reducing you to the blackbird status of a bag of bones. You lived between the waves, or at least you learned to gulp for breath between the rages sent your way by an angry god with his workboots and his whiskey. It was a life of being beaten again and again, the bite of a belt buckle slashing against the flesh of your naked back as you stood there and took it, bending now, bleeding where the buckle flays the flesh and skin. Me never really knowing why, because knowing why never made it any better.

There was no other way. A plane over Texas almost crashes and we make an emergency landing. Everyone survives. I never knew why we traveled. The truth is that the physical conflicts that arose between my father and myself took root and shape from the fact that I steadfastly refused to acknowledge the power of the demons that could drive adults. I never knew why we were always going somewhere. I was a kid. I never understood what we were traveling from or where we were traveling to. I still can't define why the adults in my family were always ready to go somewhere else. There was a wanderlust to it. It was a nomadic existence.

I once wrote a book about some of our adventures in the South once. The Florida Keys. Apalachicola. Mississippi. But the book didn't work because I was determined to give it a sense of home we never really had. Giving myself a sense of place in the context of writing was like attempting to construct a home that you knew would blow away in the violence of a hurricane. We were not immune from storms, although the storm we weathered most of all emanated from the man who was our cowboy dad.

Kids traveled light. One bag. Kids never asked why. Kids did as they were told or else. We were always going somewhere else. We were always passing through somewhere. There were other relatives to see. Other reservations. Other towns. Other folks to visit. Other adventures. It could make you dizzy going from one place to another. It could make your head spin. The train broke down in Nebraska. The bridge got washed out. And while we waited us kids ran into town. More kids than Cracker Jacks. It was exhilarating because you were afraid the train might leave without you. I was always mixed up with other children. Some family members, some not. The Navajo Nation. Chippewa shacks and eating pemmican. Indian corn hanging everywhere.

I remember hearing southern accents, but I cannot connect them to a place. In fact, even as an adult I cannot connect to place and often write what I write—my lifelines—as if place were unimportant. Even as I study how Indian stories evolve into mythologies, I find that place is something of a universal concept.

I cannot connect the dots on the map. My desk is cluttered with maps. My desk is an old plywood board held up by plastic crates. The only map that means anything is a Navajo map, and all Navajo maps are the same: Go up that hill toward the sun. Turn left at the four corners. Drive past that fence with the shoes on it. Go up that mountain past the red rocks until you get to where the lady up there keeps her sheep.

If I have followed any map at all, it is a Navajo map where the landmarks are ephemeral and sometimes shadows.

The dots on the map get washed away by rain and wind. I can tell you what was, but I cannot tell you why it was. You have to make your own deductions.

No explanation by an adult was ever offered. Kids were not important.

We lived in trucks and cars.

I remember tents. Cots.

We were the white people who lived with the brown people who lived with the red people who were all mixed up with the brown people who were surrounded by the white people (who always called the shots) who lived next to the black people who lived near the half-brown people who all had relatives in prison. It was just a fact that our world was a half-breed place of many colors and shades, and you accepted that, because there were no other options. It just was.

You never questioned the fact you were a mongrel. Not too different from them other ragged dogs chained to posts and trees.

It was not about place or race. It was about a nomadic sort of existence mixed with big quantities of survival. Color was irrelevant.

People were never simply one thing or another. People were a *mix* of things. People could be trouble, too. We once ran out of food and money and had to live on what fish I caught and brought home to cook. We never saw the world as black and white. We saw the world as something we were in, something immensely complicated. It was bigger than anyone knew. It took a long time to get from one end of it to the other. And the people in it were a mix of things, never just one color or another.

It was a shock to learn that other children did not share this vision. This otherness.

It was a shock to learn that other children saw you as either white or brown or black or whatever. You could not be a mix because mixing wasn't done.

I have only a few memories of school. My memories are snippets and images of the traveling. My memories are like a traveling slide show and a carnival.

I remember the back seats of cars. Stars and trucks.

The back of my dad's neck as we were traveling.

I do not remember Los Angeles. But I remember the rain.

I remember the snow in Michigan.

I remember the waves off Key West. Blue and crystal.

I remember the smells and tastes, but I do not have an understanding of why we were in any one particular place.

There was no why. There was only how. And the how of it was difficult enough to survive and always fleeting.

Sometimes we went to a place because my dad wanted to see it. It was that simple, even if getting there was exhausting and anything but simple. I still resist giving a name to the demons that drove him. I remember the food we ate, but I have no recollection of why we were wherever we were. Somewhere along the way I gave up trying to understand the why of it.

Until there was no why. Why was irrelevant.

My Navajo map does not explain the why of anything. What is, is.

You go up that dirt road toward the mountain until you come to where the lady up there keeps her sheep. Now that's a map I know something about.

It was everything I could do to make it through the emergency landing somewhere in Texas, the engines of the plane spitting fire, and I know there is a lot I have blotted out. There are images I do not care to remember. There are places I refuse to visit. To attempt to do so would pull me down into the vortex, and the vortex is not a place I care to recall.

I recall enough.

I can recall being beaten, but I do not care to write about it. Putting it into words won't change any of it. What was, was. Survival was something you accomplished even in the midst of family.

My parents never explained the why of much of anything. I was just a kid. What was was often overwhelming. It was my job and responsibility to accept it and get on with it and not to let any of the younger kids get lost, because when they got lost it was usually my fault. I was lost enough as it was. You could get into big trouble for ditching the younger members of the group. I was always losing them. We would find the young ones lost and crying on a path in the woods trying to get home. The group was amorphous. It was always changing. Needles, California, from a Jeepster.

Changing trains in Chicago.

High mountain lakes in Colorado.

More questions than answers.

You had to find out your own answers, and the only place

you were going to find them was in yourself. It didn't particularly matter where you were.

I cannot account for the demons of adults.

My parents did two things to ease the traveling: they told stories and they sang songs. You took home with you wherever you were. Las Vegas blacktop shimmering in the heat. Driving all night across the country and the next day and the next day and the next day and then finally stopping in a motel with a pool out by the highway.

Eating watermelon in a field and spitting out the seeds. Baling hay.

One would like to think that as an adult one did not necessarily repeat the patterns one experienced as a child.

My repetitions are my failures and my songs.

I want to focus on the good things.

I don't want to focus on the arguments and the fights between my parents. I don't want to focus on the breakdowns. I don't want to focus on my dad beating me. It's not a vacuum I care to dwell in. I don't want to focus on my dad walking out. I want the good things to blot out the bad things, and mainly they do. I don't want to think about rape or hear about it on the news.

The bad things can suck you down into a whirling vortex too dark to crawl out of.

Like an avalanche.

Carnivals. I want to focus on the carnivals.

I like the way the Ferris wheel stops when you're at or near the top. The Ferris wheel completely stops and girls get on the ride below. You can see the carny lights all the way to China.

In the car, Mother always sat up front. I do not recall ever seeing her in the back seat where us kids sat. I remember riding in a thousand vehicles. My parents aren't around to explain it all. Not that they would explain anything if they *were* around. Death is absolute and I cannot make them speak. I was a kid and so was not always owed an explanation. It was important to know how to change a tire. Mother would tell a story. Or my dad would sing a song. He knew a thousand songs, my cowboy dad. It's hard to interject yourself into the passing landscape of someone so joyous he had to sing to get it out.

It's hard to account for someone so filled with joy he could also be just as filled with rage, with an ability to hurt you.

My dad was a runaway horse.

You give up asking what comes next, because it has occurred to you that no one really knows.

Your sleeping bag, the one you share with your cousin, fits into a hundred narrow places. Fits on the floor in the back seat of cars with the popcorn, the Cracker Jacks, and the loose pennies.

Everyone clawing through the seats in search of change to pay the toll. The plane almost crashed somewhere over Texas. We made an emergency landing. I want to focus on the fact that everyone survived.

Sometimes my dad would take me into the wilderness. I do not know why he did this. Sometimes it would be just to see the stars. We'd be there in the darkness, laid out flat against some barren hill or in a canoe on a river somewhere. He always saw more shooting stars than I did. Whole oceans of them. You learned to survive and you learned not to ask so many questions, because there weren't always answers to the questions you asked.

Places had names but so did trucks and cars and dogs. My dad gave names to everything.

I have no clear vision of the past even though I was there. It comes to me in dreams and flashes, and the dreams and flashes are not necessarily connected. Although I am an adult, the dreams and flashes are just as scary as they were when I was a child. There are not always connections between the places of remembering. I wish I could say I haven't moved around like my parents did, but I have. Other kids had things. I had memories. I don't have photographs. I never kept ticket stubs. You learned to be selective about what memories you kept, what memories you threw away. You closed your eyes and hoped the plane would land. It always did. You saw fire coming from the engines. You landed in a place you did not intend to go, but you always landed. Emergencies were everywhere. Like rape.

It has never been a life of equilibrium. It was mercurial and still is.

I do not know that I can explain it outside the context of telling stories and allowing the stories to tell themselves.

I can't make all the stories connect because the connections are not always there. I cannot tell you why. The why of it eludes me. I am still too busy surviving—holding on tight while the plane's engine spits sparks into the night—to find the why of any of it. I do not know why. I only know *portions* of the how. I cannot tell you how the carnival popped up overnight. Only that it did. I can only tell you how bloodcurdling fabulous the ride was.

I do not sing songs; I have the memories of my father's voice. I do not tell stories like my mother did; I have my writing. Snippets. Flashes. Images. Dots on a map. It's all I have. I have a wife now. I am still learning about what goes into the making of a relationship. I am still learning how to stay in one place for at least a year. I can still see the carny lights all the way to China. I have all the places I have seen. I have my dog whose name is Navajo. I have what I write down and I have my vehicle.

I look like my dad but I have my mother's eyes. Brown as is the ribbed red sand.

# 5

# Chahash'oh

SOMETIMES I think I do everything wrong. This includes parenting. I wanted to introduce my young son to the magic of the wilderness. I didn't count on bears.

I was in Montana with my dog, Navajo, and my young Indian son, Tommy Nothing Fancy. I was here to write about fishing the Flathead River on the Flathead Indian Reservation. We were staying in a cabin I had rented from a Flathead Indian whose name was Sits in the Night. Sits in the Night lived in Lonepine. The cabin I had rented, built right on the banks of the river, was situated in the woods between the Mission Range and the Bitterroots. We left our pickup, Old Big Wanda, off to the side of the gravel road that more or less followed the contour of the river. I look back at the reassuring sight of Old Big Wanda. She's what gets us from A to B, and out of here if we need to go. Even though she was ancient, she ran like a charm. Something had to. We hiked into the woods toward where the cabin was supposed to be. I had not figured bears anywhere into the equation. I was thinking fish, not grizzlies.

Ignorance.

Tommy and I have to cover ourselves with vast quantities of bug dope. I put some on the dog, too. She bounds ahead of us on the trail to the cabin and the river. She is a herding dog, not a hunting dog. More heart than brains. She sniffs at bear scat.

I am thinking, Hmmm, you don't want to herd any of those.

Sits in the Night meets us at the cabin. He tells me the fishing has been good. "Bears been around," he says. I have been among Native Americans all my life, so I know understatement when I hear it. Old Stoneface and I are on a first-name basis.

Sits in the Night asks if I have packed a gun.

"Nothing that will stop a grizzly bear," I say.

The Flathead smiles. "This will stop a grizzly bear," he says. He hands me a twelve-gauge Beretta S686 Onyx shotgun. "Shells are in the cupboard. This gun won't kill a grizzly dead, you know, but it will make him reconsider."

"Reconsider what?"

"Eating you," Sits in the Night says. "The boy and the dog would be light snacks for a grizzly."

I am beginning to wonder if this trip is such a good idea.

Sits in the Night will be back at the end of the week to check on us. Chances are we won't see any other human beings for the duration of the week. This is the wilderness.

Tommy and I unpack. I make pinto bean stew. I cook the beans and slab bacon in a well-blackened cast-iron Dutch oven provided by Sits in the Night. Put the beans into the pot and cover well with water. Bring to a boil, reduce the heat, cover tightly, and simmer for a couple of hours, adding more water as needed. We got our water from the Flathead. When the beans begin to get tender, sprinkle in some salt and pepper. There are wild onions in the woods and I add them to the pot.

The smell is a deliciousness that drifts through the Flathead forest. Three grizzly bears, a mother and two cubs, show up at our cabin door.

I lock the thick pine door securely.

"They can't come inside," I tell my son. It's true. The cabin is too solid. It is built like a fortress. I put shells in the Beretta anyway and lean it in the corner by the door.

We eat our pinto bean stew while the bears paw around and snort outside. The dog barks and growls.

It has absolutely no effect on the grizzly bears.

Normally Tommy Nothing Fancy would be running around the cabin and the woods, exploring big rocks, fishing places, and the river.

But not this evening.

The next day we share the river with the bears. The mother keeps her distance. She is wary of us and the dog. I keep the Beretta leaned against a nearby tree. I keep telling myself it's good for my son to be aware of sharing the wilderness with the animals that live here. Just knowing the bears are around makes us focus more acutely on our immediate surroundings. In fact, it sort of pushes us together in odd ways.

Like you don't wander off to pee. You pee right where you are.

We try not to lose sight of each other or the dog.

The bears are better fishermen than we are. We keep one eye on them. They keep one eye on us.

You can smell them before you can see them.

You have to have respect for a grizzly bear. The cubs play in trees while their mother digs for roots. She is not all that interested in us, and I am glad.

The bears play and act like clowns. However, I am not fooled.

A mountain shadow reaches the river in late afternoon, and the cold pool we're fishing darkens suddenly. A chill breeze comes down from the peaks where there is still some snow. It is the ghost-fishing witching hour. We see a noisy run at the pool's head and a few standing waves with a deep, slow eddy at one side, a place where foot-long rainbow trout wait on big dry flies. Once a fly fisherman has become a pretty good caster, he often starts fishing with longer casts than necessary. It must have something to do with human ego. The bears literally rip the rainbow from the water, sending fish up onto the grassy banks of the Flathead, where the bears sit like fat comics eating their catch. It almost makes us want to laugh.

Big trout are not everywhere in big deeper water, and the reading of broad rivers for potential spawners becomes something of an art. There is heavy water here with barely visible submerged boulders. Mother bear sits in the middle of the flowing river seemingly oblivious to the current all around her.

I am using a frayed Silver Outcast. A hook-jawed male strikes early in the streamer's swing as it passes a nearly invisible giant boulder that seems to have its own environment of eddies, boils, standing waves, and slicks. One lunging jump and a downstream run has me stumbling and angling toward the shore. The fish has gained the attention of the bears. Throwing big streamers at big browns has become a bad and lazy habit. The mother grizzly is edging closer. She seems only to have just now realized we are here to fish. I let the big brown go. The mother bear rises on her haunches. It is time for us to retreat into our cabin.

We didn't notice the big male until the next day, when we saw him watching us and the cubs and the mother bear from a ridge overlooking the river. While she is as big as a house, he is as big as a freight train. The animal is monstrous, heavy, and well fed. I am thinking that males, females, and grizzly cubs don't mix. He heads for the river in our general direction. In his own awesome way, he is an extraordinary living thing. Grizzlies need a lot of territory.

The female grizzly sees him, too, and she scampers off into the woods with her bouncing offspring. Once again, it is time to leave the river. My son and I gather our stuff, the gun, and our dog, and we go inside. From the window of the cabin (much too small for a grizzly bear to get through) we see him move like a shadow through the trees. We call him Chahash'oh, the Navajo word for shadow. He is a towering, massive, dreadful creature.

The next day, we didn't fish. It's dangerous enough with just the mother grizzly and her cubs around, but when you add a male grizzly into the mix you have too many carnivorous possibilities. It rained anyway. We built a fire inside. It wasn't quite dark when the fighting of the bears commenced. It was that middle place of light caught between the morbid and the mystical. The musical and the misbehaved. The grizzlies weren't too far from the cabin. It wasn't something you wanted to look out the window to see. I certainly did not want Tommy to see. But I was in some strange way compelled to look, because I had to know, had to understand what was out there in the infinite moonglade darkness by the river. Moving shadows and fury.

I put the shotgun on the table. I do not know why I did this; no bear was going to get inside. Indeed, no bear had made any attempt to break into the cabin. Where we were safe. The fighting of the bears was a loud and awesome thing out there in the fanaticism of the night. Out there where the very earth was made to tremble. It made us feel very small. This was the wilderness.

This was where life and death existed side by side in the mercurial, agitated grip of robust profusion and reciprocity. This was where life and death existed side by side and neither one was a moral judgment, and grizzly bears could only be what they were.

This wasn't *Bambi*. These weren't storybook characters from the cartoon jungle. This was life and death, and man was just another shivering creature in the cave.

The bears fought on to the end. There was no other way. My son had to bury his head under his pillow. The sounds outside were fierce and roaring and frantic and filled with tameless, terrifying rage. The male grizzly killed the female and then he killed her cubs. This was the wilderness, where what is, is. The sounds of the dying female were horrible enough, but the sounds of the screaming cubs filled the universe with an unspeakable anguish I never knew existed as the babies lost their lives to the thundering carnivore that was the male grizzly.

In the morning, Chahash'oh was gone.

He did not eat the bears he had killed. He left them for other carnivores to consume.

The wilderness always takes back what it creates. The wilderness can be a generous goddess, or she can withhold her favors. She can be avaricious when she wants to be begrudging. She is hard-handed and uncharitable. It is not incumbent on life to evolve into happily ever after. Take your happilies while you can. What you have are moments. All sorts of animals from the forest came to tear and eat pieces of the bears. Animals you never knew were there. Nothing here is ever wasted.

We spent the last few days of our stay here catching rainbows. We did not see Chahash'oh again, although a few times I thought I could smell him. I kept the shotgun within arm's reach.

Sits in the Night came to get us at the end of the week. I told him the story of the bears, and he nodded silently. Sits in the Night has lived among grizzly bears all his life. Tommy and I walked through the woods to show him the bodies of the bears, but all that was left were shadows and some scattered bones.

It was time to leave the woods and return to the Desert Southwest. There are no grizzlies on the rez. There are black bears, though.

You can't see the horizon when you're in the woods. The woods are close and hide so many things. Sometimes I think I do everything wrong. Taking my son into the wilderness was a dangerous thing to do, yet the introduction had to be made.

Children do not understand the notion of respect when that notion is only articulated. Words. I wanted to be more than a man of words. Children have to see respect in action in order to imitate it. We walk to the reassuring tank of a vehicle that gets us around. Safety. Drive with your son into the gray.

*6*

# Reservation Rocks
# and the Long Walk Home

MEMORY is not enough. One needs a mythology, too.
What was can be again.

I do not have photographs of my walk with Bobby Coyote
across New Mexico. What I have are images branded inside my
crazy head. The smell of campfires. Wondering how you describe the mountains of New Mexico. Mere words fail me. The
sight of something flashing briefly in the pines. A red stand of

aspen. What you remember are dirt roads that intersect like nothing less than fabulous connections gone abandoned. Dirt roads have a shared loneliness to them. I do not have tourist mementos. What I have are images I attempt to put into words so you get the smell and the feel of the place. Place as it serves the function of telling the story.

Without my stories I am nothing. My stories branded with a flurry of images are what I am. Navajo stories can be ornate. This one is.

A Navajo story might contain the almost sardonic likes of Bobby Coyote. (This is not his real name. I am loath to offend the real Bobby Coyote. Anyway, his name isn't important. What's important is his love of life, and how that love comes coupled with responsibility.) He is a historian.

Bobby Coyote could be one of the War Twins. A coyote is regarded as a resplendent figure, worthy of great respect. Bobby is also a Vietnam veteran. A Vietnam veteran whose youth is slipping through his useful hands like water from a spring escapes through your cupped fingers as you attempt to bring it to your mouth to drink. Bobby is forever complaining that Navajo young people understand so little of their past.

"I hate to be the bearer of bad news," I told him. "But young white people aren't exactly up on history either."

Trust me.

The term "ethnic cleansing" hadn't been invented yet. Ethnic cleansing—genocide—was not invented by the Serbs. Having known Bobby for a long time now, having endured his wild youthful days, I was somewhat amused to hear him bitch about the young and what they know and do not know.

"Well, it's good to hear," Bobby observed, "that Navajo young people and white young people share something."

"*Ignorance.*" We both said it.

"The difference," Bobby maintained, "is that young white people aren't losing their culture, and young Navajo kids are losing their culture in alarming ways."

Image: the face of gang graffiti up and down the cultures of northern New Mexico. The scrawled symbols of a rape.

I understand Bobby's consternation and his anguish at cultural loss. I understand that Navajo children are losing their culture to the culture of MTV. The gangs of Los Angeles have found their way to the reservation, too. Crime—just what the reservation needs.

But what Bobby doesn't understand is that white culture isn't a culture at all. It's an *un*culture, and as such it isn't in any danger of disappearing. There's nothing there to disappear. Go poof. White culture is ephemeral. It is intolerant.

"I know Indian students who have never even heard of the Bosque Redondo," Bobby said, shaking his Navajo head. "How do you comprehend what you're up against when you have no concept of the past?"

No branded images.

It was Bobby Coyote's idea that the two of us could walk to the Bosque Redondo.

This is his idea of remembering.

Bobby refuses to admit that neither of us is getting any younger.

He is insane. He should be locked up somewhere incommunicado. Walk to the Bosque Redondo? "We could do it," he said. *We?*

We is a very dangerous word.

"I'm too old to walk to the Bosque Redondo," I attempted to explain. "I'm too fat to walk to the Bosque Redondo. I'm too arthritic to walk to the Bosque Redondo, Bobby."

Why would someone who has a nice clean job, a job with an office, the kind of job where you never get dirty, even suggest we walk to the Bosque Redondo?

Yes, Bobby Coyote is insane.

He's one of those *serious* Navajo, the kind of person who understands that he *is* his history.

"We'll have to get in shape," he said.

I could hardly wait.

I'm a writer. I have very strong fingers. I like looking out the window—don't ask me what I'm looking at—for long periods of time, thinking things. I drink strong coffee day and night. I'm a wreck. I'm allowed. If I'm not shaking my finger at someone, then I'm typing. I lead the writing life. Bobby is an academic.

Bobby Coyote showed up at my door early in the morning— every morning—for a year. "We have to run," he said. "Get into shape."

My idea was that Bobby Coyote would walk to the Bosque Redondo by himself. I would drive and meet him there, and he could tell me all about his great adventure walking across the state of New Mexico. "I'm sure you would learn a lot," I said.

"I think it would be too dangerous to walk it alone," he said. There was some truth to this. "I need you to go with me."

"Why me?" I asked.

"I thought you were a writer."

"I'm an *unpublished* writer. There's a difference."

"How many writers do you know who have experienced the Long Walk to the Bosque Redondo?"

I had to think real hard. I was pretty sure Norman Mailer has never done it.

"No one has walked to the Bosque Redondo since 1863," I pointed out.

I hate being the first to do anything. Some of this was untraveled territory.

"It will be a challenge," Bobby said.

Some historians have a real talent for understatement.

I decided to take Navajo along.

"It's a long way," she said. "Maybe we should drive."

She is a modern-day sort of dog.

We ran every morning for a year. I gave up doughnuts. Some things are just too much.

The Bosque Redondo is one of those things.

There's a limit to the lessons you can learn from history when you are forever incarcerated in an office.

Offices are very dangerous cages indeed.

The Bosque Redondo will forever be connected to the Navajo people. In 1863 the United States military called it Fort Sumner. Fort Sumner sits near the Pecos River in De Baca County, in east-central New Mexico. The area contains some of the most desolate landscape in North America.

The story of the Long Walk Home begins with Kit Carson and ends in a description of a tribe coming to terms with its historic self. The Navajo — the Diné — remember. They tell many stories. How the U.S. military thought the entire Navajo tribe could be rounded up and marched here and how the Navajo were supposed to survive remains to this day *the* question that must be asked when exploring the reality of the Bosque Redondo.

You are your history.

Ethnic cleansing comes in many forms.

The Bosque Redondo was a concentration camp, the final solution to the problem of the Diné. No white person objected to the reality of genocide. The Navajo would be worn down, run down, frozen, starved, and forced to march to the Bosque Redondo, where the winters were deadly cold, the summers deadly hot. For thousands of Diné, it was the end.

In my memory, the place is perhaps more hypnotic than it was at the time we were there. Our biggest problem walking there was not the heat. It was not the distance. It was dehydration. We had to really watch the liquid intake. This included the dog, who had to drink too. She was such a trouper I didn't mind sharing my canteen with her.

One slow step at a time.

No photographs were ever taken of the Bosque Redondo that tell its story. It is a place history seems to have swallowed up in an apathy that existed then and an apathy that exists today, notwithstanding military involvement. The answer to the question that must be asked when exploring the reality of the Bosque Redondo is that *the Navajo were not expected to survive*. Navajo who could not keep up were shot. Navajo who attempted to escape were shot. Navajo who refused to worship the white man's god were hanged as an example to the others.

I know this from stories that were passed down by the Navajo. Navajo stories are long and often lurid. There is the story of Changing Woman. There is the story of Sa (old age). I do not know these things about the Bosque Redondo from history or from maps. A Navajo map extends itself to the third mesa, where you take the ninth dirt road to the left and walk five miles to the three stones, past the hogan, and straight up the face of a mountain until you get to where the lady up there has sheep. That is a Navajo map, and that is how the Navajo tell stories.

I know the story of the Bosque Redondo by listening to a series of recorded observations shared in loss by the Navajo. I do not know all the stories of those who were left behind, but I know they have stories, too. Their story is the starvation story, and I believe it. What happened at the Bosque Redondo would be unimaginable today. The Navajo see themselves as the People who walk the surface of the earth. When you get right down to it, that is what we're about—not ethnic cleansing, but people intent upon immediate survival and beyond. Navajo mythology remains the story of themselves. It is a story that has yet to be discovered by white Americans.

White People Town hasn't yet been able to penetrate the real complexity and truth in Navajo myth. The Navajo have always been very poor. And it has always been their culture that has seen them through such tragedies as ethnic cleansing. But the Navajo have survived. Now, there's a story in there somewhere. A richness.

Navajo sings tell stories, too.

The Navajo are themselves a culture.

One of the things I liked best about living on the big rez was how the tribe would purchase clothing for the children before the onset of winter. New clothes for school, too. New shoes sometimes. Jackets. There was no reason for a Navajo child to go cold. The Navajo can see themselves as flourishing when in fact it can be very hard being Navajo. It all begins in school. Traditionally—some traditions die harder than others—schools were places you went to live. When I lived close to a school, down the dirt road (it was usually more mud than dirt, and there was a sea of it), it had a dorm.

Consider this: there is no such thing as leftover food in a Navajo school.

· · ·

To this day, there is still much stigma attached to a Navajo who comes into contact with white men. Navajo who come into contact with white men must be cleansed.

The white part of me will always wrestle with this.

There will never be a resolution to the struggle.

I am constantly being told that I cannot be both white and Navajo.

Trust me. I can be both. I am a migrant. A mongrel. A crow.

The only thing I never expected to find on my walk to the Bosque Redondo with Bobby Coyote were human bones. There are bones along this trail of tears. Human skulls. Teeth. Jawbones. Femurs. We left them where we found them.

Old and bleached.

Perhaps they were simply other predators' bones come to the surface of the mud. At Mariano Lake the Navajo called it the Big Mud.

Navajo women were raped by soldiers.

You will find Navajo to be many colors, sometimes dark, sometimes light. Miss Navajo was half black. She was a real beauty. Again, you are your history.

The earth is littered with the historic remains of the Navajo. The fields, orchards, houses, hogans, and livestock of the Diné were systematically destroyed. Many of the displaced died of exposure, starvation, and disease. Many were executed.

The Navajo were to be civilized. They would learn farming and worship as Christians.

The landscape around Fort Sumner did not lend itself to farming. The landscape around Fort Sumner lent itself to graves.

So many Navajo perished, it soon became obvious that the

government's plan had failed. In 1868 a new treaty was negotiated, and the Navajo were allowed to return to what is now their reservation. The Navajo refer to this period of their history as the Long Walk Home.

It was a time of many stories. Stories that have the full potential of making it all the way to myth.

At the end of the Long Walk Home there remained fewer than 10,000 members of the tribe. It took many years for the Navajo to recover. Today there are more than 200,000 Diné. The Bosque Redondo and the Long Walk Home are now the stuff of stories and the past.

You are your history in ways you cannot even know.

Bobby Coyote and I would have it better than the Navajo who were forced to march all the way to the Pecos River. We had hiking boots, freeze-dried food, maps, sleeping bags, a tent, rain gear, flashlights, dry socks, matches, spare batteries, backpacks, a tiny cooking stove, canteens, and binoculars. Sometimes we had only a vague concept of where we were. Wherever we were, though, we were headed in the direction the Navajo had been forced to march, but the Navajo had been forced to march without all the modern techno-implements of hiking and survival. Insect repellent. L. L. Bean. I carried high-protein dog food. There are more fences now than when the Navajo walked to the Bosque Redondo. But in many ways much of the walk has to be the same. Vast portions of the trail suggest that very little has changed in 140 years.

The landscape on the way to the Bosque Redondo runs the gamut from jagged lava flows to vast mesas of sage. In this barren place horses arrive from over the distant hills.

The Bosque Redondo itself is devoid even of horses.

Many Navajo people have in the past visited the Bosque Redondo. It is a day's drive from the Navajo Nation. Many of the Navajo who come here bring rocks from the reservation, which they leave behind as if to say, *This is where we come from.* Symbolism.

My rock is smooth granite. Bobby's rock is red sandstone.

The first leg of our journey took us from Hosta Butte to El Morro. It took three days to walk the first forty miles. Not bad for two old geezers and a canine. The writer and the historian. It was madness. The dog was having fun. Like I said, it's the writing life. The trail here is either up or down. Nothing is flat in this section of New Mexico. There were many times I wished we had brought a mule along. The blisters on my feet were awful.

We arrived at Inscription Rock in early June. From here we walked across the lava flows of El Malpais. The lava flows tear the hell out of our hiking boots, and I wonder how the Navajo did it in moccasins or barefoot. We catch the sacred trail that runs between the Acoma Pueblo and the Zuni Pueblo. The trail has existed for at least a thousand years and has remained unchanged. We rest at the home of Ray Redshoes in Acoma for several days. There was no rest for the Navajo on the Long Walk—you kept up or you were killed. Many of the adults carried children. It is in this place of jagged rocks as sharp as razor blades and a beating sun that one begins to develop an appreciation for the courage of the People forced to march through this seething geologic hell.

From Acoma we walk to the Isleta Pueblo on the Rio Grande. We have been on Indian land now almost all the way.

We have to swim across the river. You can't do this and not wonder how children and the elderly made it across the Rio Grande alive.

We cross the Cibola National Forest and follow a railroad track east of Willard. There are no people here. There are ruins of a mission (I do not know the name of this mission or if it even had a name, but I do remember the heat) where the Navajo were forced, many of them for the first time, to worship the Christian god, who is male. This was a shock to the Diné, whose principal deity, Changing Woman, is female. You got down on your knees or you were shot. The Navajo had never bent their knees to anyone. "On your knees" means the same thing in any language.

The land becomes bleak and dry — drier than what we have crossed already, which is hard to imagine, but here it is. The immediate image of the land is one of total flatness surrounded by desert mountains, but like most images, the flatness is an illusion like the shimmering from the heat. There are plenty of arroyos, and they must be negotiated. This is where you are most likely to trip and fall and twist an ankle. What we think is Pedernal Mountain rises in the distance.

The mountains slow us down. Even the clouds overhead seem dry. We cross Guadalupe County. In our small tent at night, muscles I didn't know I had pleaded with me to stop this nonsense. I'm too old. I'm too fat. I'm too decrepit for this insanity. There are gaps in my memory of that pain today. I know my blisters screamed objections. Bobby Coyote's philosophy: If our ancestors did it, we can do it too.

The dog agrees.

The earth never seemed to end. There is an oceanic quality to the terrain. The Navajo must have known they were entering Comanche territory. The Comanches were fearless enemies and one of the reasons the Navajo lived where they did. You are being marched by one enemy into the heart of the territory of another. Most Navajo must have thought they were marching to certain death.

De Baca County seems filled with rattlesnakes. At night there is the howling of coyotes. "My family was marched here," Bobby says. I say nothing. I am too exhausted to talk. "It's a mistake to assume it could never happen again."

Anyone who studies the language of the Navajo, Athabaskan, confronts the reality of conceptual repetition.

What was can be again.


Most of my distant ancestors — the people my mother claimed to come from — managed to evade the bluecoats. Not all. The Navajo who managed to escape the wrath of Kit Carson, the rapes, the murders, the night of the long knives, came to be called Those Who Hid Away. It's hard to hide away when you know your children are being butchered.

It was very hard on the Navajo.

The People who walk the surface of the earth were very brave indeed.

Petroglyphs on the walls of Cañon del Muerto tell the story of the Spanish driving out the Navajo. It was a story that would be repeated.


The landscape of the Bosque Redondo can only be described as unforgiving. There is no water here. What water we have is what water we have. The biggest challenge is to avoid becoming one with the surrounding dryness. We drink and we drink. The rainstorm we anticipated turned to hail. There is no water to capture in falling hail. The train tracks lead us across Conejos Mesa all the way to the highway and then Fort Sumner.

Memories of specific events fade as all memories fade and blur over time. How could you not know you would write about the Navajo and fail every time you did? There are many tourists here. Recreational vehicles. Campers. Sport utility vehicles hauling Airstreams. Lost white people in search of the Old West who have come to take pictures of the grave of Billy the Kid.

Billy the Kid is white people mythology. Billy was supposedly a rebel. Now he is myth, too.

I find a Coke machine. I make one appear before me like a glowing shrine to sanity.

We drink and we drink again. We have walked four hundred miles, and we look it. The bleak landscape feels like an echo from somewhere else. There is little to remind one that the entire Navajo tribe was marched here, where so many of them died.

I did it.

I remember bones at the side of the trail.

I remember horses on the way.

I remember Auschwitz and how it looks so much like the rest of the Polish countryside. Auschwitz in those picture books at school. In the final analysis, both Auschwitz and the Bosque Redondo are ordinary places.

Kosovo is ordinary, too.

I look forward to spending the night in a motel.

I would kill for clean sheets and a shower.

Ray Redshoes meets us in his truck. Ray laughs and says we look like shit. Bobby and I will drive back to the Navajo Nation where we live. I am glad not to have to walk.

I'm not sure I could have walked this route again.

Bobby Coyote leaves his red piece of sandstone on a large

pile of rocks left here by other Navajo. I leave my piece of granite. Not too far away from this pile of rocks is a Park Service sign that commemorates the Bosque Redondo. The large pile of rocks left here does not look unlike a grave. Symbolism.

Alone at night when the wind kicks up out here on the mesa of the Bosque Redondo, you can hear the singing voices of ghosts. The Bosque Redondo is a past that runs like blood through a river of my dreams.

There are no wild horses here.

You are your history.

What was can be again.

I no longer drive around the reservation with the same take-it-for-granted feeling. Now I can feel the footsteps. And sometimes I can hear them, humming along in some kind of haunting resonance with Old Big Wanda's engine. Like running moccasins. Fast through the smell of pine. The presence of the old ones will be with me every time I take a step. *Nishli nil*—I am with you.

# 7

# Tenderloin

/ HAVE LIVED in the Tenderloin district of San Francisco. Tens of thousands of people live here; it has always been a crowded place. The Tenderloin is not a place of symbolism.

All the Glide Church hymns of holy ghosts and grails revolted in their steadfast grudges like some amorphous thing come in out of the monster shadows of the cosmos to gorge itself, struggling and gasping on the morsels of the concrete void. That is the Tenderloin.

I know her fatal, sucking black holes like I know her treacheries. But this time I was only visiting.

As a Mental Health Poster Child, I keep a loaded .45 handgun under my pillow in the bed of my pickup, Old Big Wanda. I am writing this in longhand, parked on Jones Street in the Tenderloin.

Not all Indians live on reservations. Some Indians are urban Indians, and the urban experience is always something of a struggle and a mystery.

More and more Indians leave the reservation to live in cities. Life on the reservation can be hard. But that very different life in the city is never, ever easy. You can lose your way in either place, and there are always those ditches, those sucking black holes, my mother claimed were so familiar. The urban lines and the hyphens and the landmarks of our lives are like features of a moon of cloven hooves. The police do not come when called for emergency assistance when such quaint notions as domestic violence and loud noise and the sound of gunshots occur anywhere in the Tenderloin. The Tenderloin is a reservation too, and there is nothing people here love to do more than simply walk around and see how people live who are better off than they are. Urban Indians refuse to live up to the stereotypes they are assigned. The same goes for reservation Indians, but they're too remote to know about it.

As I write this it is night, but Jones Street is crowded with hookers, pimps, Marin County businessmen in slowly passing cars, screaming junkies with their blackened empty eyes, the homeless with their newspaper shoes and shopping carts, Vietnamese children playing on the sidewalk, Chicano gang boys drifting in and out of apartment buildings, drag queens in their lipstick and heels, thick blue smoke from a Korean steak house, belching buses pulling up, the squeal of brakes, the steam-cover smell of sewage fog dancing in the gutters.

Boots crunching needles and watch where you walk.

Boom box rapping daddy shakes the concrete and the stones and bones and moans wrapped in all this bloody tissue that is human.

Sometimes street people come by and sit on the hood of my truck until they realize someone is in there and then they leave. I try not to shoot them.

I play my Navajo flute back here in Old Big Wanda, and somehow it helps keep the Tenderloin at bay — even more perhaps than the comforting presence of my gun. For without our sacred eagle's battle cries, our awkward Indian timidities — our sad politeness — give the light that spills a hideous blindness, and no emphasis is put on the strangulating rope that whites have slipped around our supple throats. Let the Indian look to himself.

Here in San Francisco, I write poems in burger joints. Hamburger Mary's. Hardee's. Jack in the Box. You can still buy a burger for a buck. "Do you like poetry?" I ask people in these places. No one is wise enough to say no. I hand them some of my poems. Sometimes they hand me a dollar. Sometimes five. Usually it's enough to buy a burger. Poetry feeds me. And feeds my soul, too.

I walk my dog, Navajo, down Post Street to Union Square, the only bit of green around here, where she can pee. I pee also, in an underground toilet in a parking garage where men are having sex and they don't care who sees.

One sees many things in the Tenderloin. Sitting in the Boom Boom Room watching rain drip down through the savage wreckage of my life. The Tenderloin will always claim me. It will always find me. And my soul, with its quarantines, its criteria, and its prefigurements, a victim of its own picturesque vernacular.

I have driven to the Tenderloin at the request of two close friends, both Sioux, both women, who live on the Pine Ridge Reservation in South Dakota. The three of us go back about a thousand years. Old flames become lasting friendships. Both women have sons. Their sons are seventeen, and some time ago the sons ran away to San Francisco. Running away to San Francisco was neither original nor creative. There are men who truly believe they must make their mark against the earth but find themselves instead being chased by some leper pariah through the landscapes of lasting rages. A pilgrimage. I am here to find these boys if only to report back to their mothers, both of whom are worried sick.

Light another cigarette. Your sons are okay.

Okay being relative, of course.

I can see my two friends now, smoking cigarettes on the couch, talking on the phone, shaking that long, flowing Sioux hair. I would have married both of them for their hair alone. But they won't have me, and laugh at me and call me a jackass. They, too, have made their mark upon the world, in sounds of faint and fragile softness. Cleansed by all their contradictions. The smell of fry bread off somewhere. Kids with bikes outside. A basketball net nailed to a tree. Smoking. Worrying. Talking up a storm. Afraid. Still wondering about whom to consult. No medicine men here. These women miss their old mothers. It's hard being a mother. That, too, is a pilgrimage.

I know these boys, although it is their mothers I am long-term friends with. It is not all that difficult to find them. How many Sioux adolescent boys could there be in the Polk Street sex scene? How many Indian hustlers do you know? Not many. I know this: adolescents are given to illusions of loyalty, but all it takes is twenty bucks to get a friend to rat on the boys and tell me where they live. I find them easily.

You almost have to be one to find one. I knew that if I sat near the window of the Boom Boom Room, eventually they would come along. Then I would follow them, track them down, confront them if I had to. I fully suspected they would know in their bones that they were being followed the minute I turned up anywhere near Polk Street. But I found them because they had left their mark like a smeared stain all the way to Marin. Like a small river wanders through dreams of being chased. After all, they were Sioux. You take it everywhere. It goes where you go, and you push yourself to be proud of it. But it requires effort. You're just someone who wants a nice car and a nice television and running water with a toilet and the good fortune to either live or not live — it's your choice — anywhere near the reservation.

You want MTV.

The closest your life has come so far (you do not have running water, and the toilet is outside) to what television said was how white people lived, the dynamics of the situation comedy, was when you had known and brushed up against two other Sioux men who had robbed a convenience store and got away with forty dollars. Forty dollars was a lot of money. Everyone got a laugh out of that one. No one got charged with anything, because white people think all Indian men look alike. Disparaging both culture and character in a process that demeans everyone.

You still want nice things but sometimes you give up hope for them.

The two boys, Kuau-a and Tyuoni, live in a one-room dump

in a Tenderloin hotel. They have become somewhat popular among white men who prefer Asian hustlers, but a Sioux seventeen-year-old is seen as more exotic. The boys work the phones—to even have a phone here is a sign of prosperity— which is a step up from working the street. They have sex ads in San Francisco's gay paper, the *Bay Area Reporter.* You could call the two of them lovers, but since everything about their lives is dysfunctional, I'm not sure the term "lovers" would be accurate. They are indeed affectionate with each other, but I don't think they have sex together because sex is seen as something you do for money to survive. I think they're really straight. I thought my reception might be cold, but I am mistaken.

I say I am their mothers' friend. I apologize for showing up at their door.

They forgive me, and then they want to know how their moms are.

"Fine," I tell them. They scrutinize me closely. "Fine" probably means drunk as usual.

Their moms were never sober. Their dads were always beating them. The reservation high school they dropped out of was a crock of shit. So they ran away. It is a familiar story.

Now both of them are heroin addicts.

It's the night itself scratching its claws against the glass, demanding to be let out.

Now they are the monsters they used to fear when as little boys they had bad dreams and their mothers put their cards down, disrupting the poker game we'd been playing. Bad dreams by the small river that wanders through the soul. And it's your mother who comes in with her long hair, smelling of cigarettes and party, and it's your mother who rubs your back, you in your underwear with the sheet pulled up. If you're very, very lucky you might seduce her into telling you a long and involved Indian story, the kind that takes forever to tell. I always had to drag the mothers back to the poker table, admonishing them not to spoil their sons. They'd push me away, laughing, boisterous, yet with a faint and fragile softness.

You wouldn't know this on your knees, having oral sex with Sioux boys — which they get thirty bucks for — because it's not a part of them you would ever be allowed to see. It gets deep and scary out there alone without any of your own people. The men who pay them to have sex, their regulars, who think they know them, do not know anything about them, such as the fact that both boys are extremely depressed. I show them pictures of their mothers I took in Pine Ridge. We go out to dinner at the Thai Stick, on the corner of Post and Jones. They are quiet in their sadness. They are also high. It is the only way they can get through doing what they do.

I am making moral judgments here.

Except for the fact that heroin addiction is neither a morality nor a judgment. It is just the way things are.

I see their lifestyle as a death sentence.

"We can't go back," they say.

I say nothing. They shoot up in a toilet stall in the bathroom. Go back to work the phones.

I am not here to save them. They can only save themselves. I am here only to let them know someone still cares about them. It is not a complex message.

You can't scratch their backs anymore and make it better, scaring the monsters off the page.

They are not little boys, but their naiveté takes my breath away.

I spend the night in the back of my truck and play my Navajo flute. In the morning I take them to breakfast. I am surprised to see Tyuoni was beat up, black and blue, cut and swollen. He is on the verge of tears. Apparently he went out on a call in the middle of the night and was robbed and assaulted. I hesitate to use the term "rape," because the stereotype of the hustler at work is that he wants to get raped, which is hardly ever true. How difficult can it be to rape a seventeen-year-old whose only other urban experience was a visit to a mall in Sioux Falls? I buy the two Sioux boys breakfast at a small place on the corner of Jones and Sutter. They smoke Camels and try to look older than they are.

There really isn't much to say. They should be in high school, playing football and running track and preparing themselves for college.

They do not write poetry.

I give them the phone number of a detox program for adolescents in the Tenderloin.

"But they've never had anyone Sioux," Kuau-a says. He is defensive.

Sometimes you have to listen to their nightmares. And you have to sit close to them, offering them what comfort you can, wiping their tears away with a Kleenex. Other pilgrimages. You tell them it was all a dream. You will always see them as children, and there it is. There is really nothing either you or they can do to change this erroneous perception.

They will always be children to you. You only pretend to see them as all grown up, which is very much an act done primarily for their benefit.

Like most adolescent boys, Kuau-a has a high opinion of what he knows. He knows that the message I am attempting to bring them is one of hope.

"No, you're wrong," I tell him. "The counselor I talked to was Sioux. Check it out."

The counselor I had talked to told me he sees such boys every day. "Tell them," he had said, "the street is going to kill them. They will already know this, but sometimes it helps to hear it from someone else."

"The street is going to kill you," I tell them.

They know.

It is needle exchange day. We walk down to Glide Memorial Church's parking lot, where junkies gather to exchange their used needles for clean ones. We glide down to Glide like the gliding streets themselves are paved with nothing more than oil. The buzz is that the program may have to end. Health and Human Services is under orders from the White House to end government financial support for such programs. Kuau-a and Tyuoni are given a box of new needles, which will last another week.

We drive to the beach with the dog, and the three of us run her. For a brief instant the boys seem so normal. So seventeen. I take pictures of them to show their moms. Tyuoni's black eye almost disappears behind his smile. They seem so nonchalant. "Tell our moms we're okay," they said.

They are not okay.

Heroin addiction is like an animal in your belly.

When the animal comes out, it scratches and it claws.

I drop them off at their Tenderloin hotel. Time to work the phones.

"Don't forget to call that detox program," I say. "The counselor is a Sioux."

As if this means anything. Perhaps it does. I do not know.

Dance the dance, Crazy Shoes, of disconnected realms. Destroyed sweetly by the madness for all the angry fixes. Dance the choreography of small, empty hotel rooms, leaking still-

born, warships on the street, and even the gutter with its sol-
dierly combat sings strategical guerrilla, while all the dogs of
war imbrue their hands in urban blood. Misfits and junkies.
Hookers. Pimps. Businessmen from Marin in slowly passing
cars. The homeless with their newspaper shoes and shopping
carts. Vietnamese children playing on the sidewalk. Chicano
gang boys drifting in and out of apartment buildings. Drag
queens in their lipstick and heels. The pure, the virtuous, and
the blissfully deranged. The dying and the demented. Navajo
and I drive across the Golden Gate Bridge. Escape. I can
breathe again. Fog is the song of the stars in a shattered echo
rolling silently beneath the bridge. Dance the Sun Dance,
Crazy Shoes, of warriors on the street. Dance the Sun Dance,
Crazy Shoes, of rapping daddy's drumming beat. Needles,
blow jobs, and giving birth to animals.

Sometimes all of us sail too near the wind. We move in slow
reflection like cigarette smoke drifts and death flows serene beyond the superficial, polymorphous, plastic reach of splendor.
Poems or guns? Old Sioux flames that seem to shake their hair
and writhe in some angry objection to the plastic totem poles of
God. The reservation is an idea more than it is a place. Some
Indians live in the world.

All horses are runaways.

Leaving marks upon the earth.

## 8

# To the Drum

*H*WII' SIZIINII lives in a hogan just down the reservation dirt road I used to live on and he has been my friend for many years. Hwii' was born to the Reed Big Water People Clan, for the Towering People Clan, and he is a Navajo singer and a dancer. Hwii' has studied the dances of many tribes. In the summer he travels all over the West and dances at intertribal powwows.

Hwii' Siziinii is thirty. His hogan is usually a chaotic mess because he's always either repairing a dancing costume or making a new one. Buckskin, beads, and feathers are everywhere. This is a place of great creativity. "Costume" is perhaps the wrong word, implying a theatrical form of entertainment. Indian dances have much more to do with participation than with entertainment.

The purpose of many Indian dances is to symbolize participation by a human being in a natural (or supernatural) world not of his design. White people often think the purpose of Indian dancing is to entertain white people. They applaud. They throw dimes. They watch the dances as they might watch a European concert or a Broadway play. Indian dances were not created for the entertainment of white people. Indian dances are what symbolize to Indians the beauty of the cultures.

And beyond.

Hwii' Siziinii is my teacher.

The first dance he ever took me to was the Hopi Snake Dance. We drove to Shungopavi on the Hopi Indian Reservation. The Hopi people believe their Snake Dance brings them rain. According to Hopi mythology, Flute Chief, a deity, was the younger brother of the Snake Youth, who brought the Snake Dance to the people.

The Hopi Reservation lies smack in the middle of the Navajo Nation. The relationship between the Hopi and the Navajo has always been tenuous at best. At the time the boundaries of Indian reservations were being drawn up, it was common practice for the federal government to contain one reservation inside another. The reason the government did this was to foment strife among Indians. (The Arapaho, for example, share the Wind River Reservation with the Shoshone.) The Navajo and the Hopi have had many disagreements about who owns what pieces of the land. Yet the two peoples do try to get along.

It is not unusual for the Hopi to invite the Navajo to their dances. It is not unusual to see some Hopi at Navajo ceremonies.

The Hopi pueblos can trace their snake cults back to their trading relationships with the Indians of Mexico and Central America. No Indian tribe exists in total isolation from other Indian tribes. White tourists who have witnessed the Hopi Snake Dance often do not understand that what they've seen is only one small part of an elaborate ritual. The Snake Dance actually lasts sixteen days.

This is more time than most white people have to watch.

The Hopi believe they originated in an underworld. Hopi spirits still dwell Down There. Snakes are the brothers of the Hopi people, and they carry prayers to the Rainmakers beneath the earth.

The Hopi people do not allow photographs to be taken of the Snake Dance. Published photos of the Snake Dance are frauds.

The rattlesnakes are deadly. They are skillfully handled by dancers who carry them in their hands and in their mouths.

Carrying your life and your god in your mouth is a powerful symbol. Carrying a rattlesnake in your mouth extricates you from the separation of the People from the earth and connects you to the cosmic.

The dancer dances to keep from falling into a blackness he knows is there gnawing at his bones like an animal. A gravity to all his many failures. Yet no one is a failure here. In dancing you leave all of that behind, and not even the dead can catch you.

A week before the public dance, the Snake Priests collect snakes from the desert. The first day they go north. The second day they go west. The third day they go south. The fourth day they go east. Their bodies are painted red, and except for loin-cloths they are naked. The nakedness is itself important, be-cause it is the nakedness that is a request for rain to cool their sunburned bodies. The Hopi Snake Dance would never receive the official seal of approval from the White People's Family Val-ues Council. Do not bring white children to see it. Republicans should stay home. Christians should stay away. Leave the Hopi to their snakes and their religion. Here nakedness is a symbolic prayer. No one on the Hopi Reservation is shocked to see the nakedness of men.

On the fifteenth day of ceremonies, an Antelope People race is held. Anyone may participate. Many do. The racers represent the rain gods bringing water to the village.

When the race is finished, the Antelopes gather green boughs and build a *kisi*, a simple structure that provides shade, and in front of the *kisi* the Hopi dig a shallow pit. This is the en-trance to the underworld. At sunset the Antelope Dancers emerge from their kiva. The rattles they shake are the sound of rain.

The Snake Chief makes a medicine of roots. The snakes are washed, because they are the children of the Hopi. It is believed that if the snakes are washed they will send rain to wash the earth.

Pink clay is smeared on moccasins, arms, calves, and the up-per right side of the dancers' heads. Chins are painted white. The rest of the face is painted black.

The snakes are deposited in the *kisi*, and the Antelope Dancers scatter meal among them. There is much singing. The Snake Priests carry snakes in their hands, then around their necks, then in their mouths. Holding a snake in your teeth is a powerful form of prayer. Each snake is danced four times around the plaza. The priests release the snakes, then bathe in the root medicine that has been brewing all day. The Snake Priests then drink the medicine. All this will cause the rains to come.

For the Hopi, the snake is a symbol of wisdom and sexual power. The antelope, in contrast, represents the feminine, the timid, the elusive, and the subtle among those of us who inhabit the surface of the earth.

I cannot bring myself to put a rattlesnake in my mouth. I would be a failure as a Hopi.

Hwii' Siziinii laughs. "I will teach you how to do it," he says.

I know he will.


Hwii' teaches me many of the dances. We dance outside his hogan in our skins.

The Navajo do not call them dances. The Navajo call them sings.

"Navajo" is a Tewa word meaning "cultivated area."

You are your history.

The Night Chant lasts nine days. Hwii' Siziinii calls this ceremony the Yeibichai. The Yei are gods. The Yeibichai is the Grandfather of the Gods. Grandfather and his mate are both portrayed by men. The Yeibichai mask that Grandfather wears is of white buckskin, has red and yellow hair and a fan of eagle feathers across the top from ear to ear. Little boys are initiated with sacred meal and whipped with yucca whips by the Yei. Sometimes the little boys cry, but the crying never lasts long. It is good to hear them wail with their healthy lungs. Children are allowed to wear the masks so they too might feel like gods.

The Yeibichai's mate does not come out at night, for evil spirits are about.

Dancers have rattles, and spruce twigs are held below the

knees. There is much mirth and laughter as we dance. The dancing connects us to one another and to the earth, who is our mother. Here all of us are brothers, lifting and stamping our right feet. *Huu! Huu! Huu!* The gods decline to speak to men in human languages.

The dancing men are nearly naked. The upper halves of our bodies are smeared with gray paint.

We too have mates. They are portrayed by other male dancers. We dance until the sun rises over Hosta Butte. We stamp with power and sing in clear, loud voices the last song of the Ycibichai. In beauty it is finished.

When you are dancing you feel alive. You are participating in something beyond the concept of a culture. You are allowed for a short while to be caught in that middle place between culture and what is beyond the reach of man.

To the drum. To the drum.

We dance the Sioux Horse Dance. We dance the Ghost Dance, which was forbidden for many years because it breathed the breath of fear into the mouths of white men. Full regalia. War shirts. Leggings. War bonnets. Sun Dance buffalo skulls. Porcupine hair roaches. Fox Dance. Horse Dance. Scalp Dance. Fire Dance. Grass Dance. We dance in White People Town at the Indian Cultural Center (which is the Amtrak station), where the white tourists applaud and throw their dimes.

I don't see them. They aren't there. I blot them out.

Life is dancing. Dancing is life.

You are your history.


I usually walk from my hogan to Hwii' Siziinii's hogan. I never drive. The reservation dirt road smells of hot dry air, and sunflowers grow profusely in the ditch. Today I take my time, though. My dog comes along. She loves to stop and smell the sunflowers in the ditch.

Hwii' Siziinii keeps the rattlesnake in a burlap bag. The snake wants out.

*Chtchtchtchtchtchtcht.*

The dog growls some.

Hwii' pets the snake and calms it.

"Remember," he says. "Your teeth are your prayer."

Dancing is the blood that runs like a river through my dreams.

Tomorrow I will dance among the Hopi.

We will drive to the ancient Hopi Pueblo — built when white people believed the earth was flat — in Old Big Wanda. We won't say much on the way to Shungopavi. The dance will be our words. And the tongue speaks languages of dust.

# 9

# Half-and-Half

W̶E DANCED around the campfire to the sound of perpetual drums. The sand painting had been returned to dust. The drums had been played in that way Indians play their drums, so that even when the drums were not being played you could still hear them in the rhythmic spaces inside your head. Some Navajo smile when they see me. There is a welcome in their smiles. They do not know that my mother was a Navajo. Or so she claimed. I look like my dad. My dad was white. The smiles are warm but mostly it's Old Stoneface. I have tried for years to figure out a way to make Old Stoneface into a friend. I succeed only about one time in ten. Old Stoneface cracks and I get a smile. But the crack in the persona has to begin with me. Old Stoneface, he don't crack too easily. Sometimes it takes a hammer and a chisel. Mainly his façade is as hard as Apache granite.

Old Stoneface is like a cup of coffee that is too hot to drink. You hold the thing in your hand and you wait. Sometimes you mix in half-and-half to cool it down. Old Stoneface does go mellow every now and then. You hit those soft spots. Even Old Stoneface has them.

Indians have a distinctly mellow place, but sometimes it's hard to scratch down to it.

My dog, Navajo, and I attend a powwow in Window Rock, Arizona. Actually, it's a Blessing Way healing ceremony, where the sacred rock arches like a window onto another reality. Another lifetime. Another world. I use the term "powwow" here so as to admit whites with their limited understanding, their limited access to Indian spirituality, their limited awareness of Navajo culture.

Whites are always welcome at Navajo ceremonies, even if their presence is rare. At such events white people for the first time *understand,* extending themselves beyond what the Navajo have come to think of as the whites' numb existence. When this happens, it amazes even Old Stoneface.

The white tourists mainly stop and take pictures. They have no concept of how they themselves are seen. The Navajo are offended by this picture-taking when permission has not been obtained, but the offense is mostly ignored.

I have seen tribal officials confiscate cameras, though, and this causes a scene. Europeans have a particularly hard time understanding this. What to them is unusual is ordinary to the Navajo. Nevertheless, one must ask permission of the person being photographed. Yes, perhaps payment would be appropriate. Old Stoneface might seem sour to the non-Indian, but you have to respect him for who he is.

Put another way: you're on the rez here. Indians call the shots.

Often, after such ceremonies I feel a little giddy. Lightheaded. All that hypnotic singing and dancing. I decide to stop for a cup of coffee. Navajo and I pull Old Big Wanda into a McDonald's parking lot.

I do not get out of the truck immediately.

Nothing immediate happens after such a sing.

I sit there in my whiteness, trying to make sense of what I have seen, tasted, danced, sang. This part of who I am has to understand what it has just experienced. I have to put it into a context. I will probably write about it. I am never able to let it just *be*.

I was more than a little amused to note the participation of a Catholic priest at the Blessing Way. No one asked the priest to explain himself. His presence was silently accepted, although there were lots of eyes. Navajo eyes. Stoneface eyes. Curious eyes that ask questions. The questions are hardly ever articulated because the Navajo usually know the answers. Question: Why would a Catholic priest participate in a pagan ritual with the savages? Answer: It adds something to that which is missing, a wholeness, an acceptance that there is more here than what we see.

"Are we done here?" Navajo wants to know. She's been a good girl for several days.

Wherever there are Navajo, you'll find Navajo dogs. I used to wonder why there were so many dogs at reservation schools until I realized they were waiting for the children they belonged to so they could walk the children home. I have never been to a Navajo ceremony where there weren't at least a few dogs loitering in the shadows.

There is no such thing as a pure-bred Navajo dog. Navajo dogs are mongrels. Mine is.

I am a mongrel myself. That mix of the morbid, the mystical, and the misbehaved.

"We're not done here. Not quite yet," I tell her. "I'm going inside McDonald's for a cup of coffee."

It was a long drive back to Mariano Lake, where we lived on the rez. I could still hear the Navajo singing and the drums in my head.

I had to clear the cobwebs. The Navajo part of me wanted to cling to the ritual of the sing. The white part of me wanted a cup of coffee. Dogs cannot go inside the Window Rock McDonald's and other designated places. No dogs allowed. She sighs and puts her head down on the front seat of the pickup. "Just don't forget about us out here," she tells me.

"I'll be right back," I tell her.

Such a baby.

The service is really bad. I have to wait a long time.

Meanwhile, Navajo standing behind me in line are waited on.

I know what's going on. I've lived with it all my life. The Navajo teenagers who work here think I'm a white person passing through. Well, I *am* passing through, but I resent being seen as pure white. Or pure anything. Purity is a fetish. I talk to them in Navajo. They seem surprised. They were going to give me a hard time, and don't know if the joke's on them or me.

Perhaps the joke is on us both. Once again, language is the

bridge over a barrier, like the sacred arches are really rocks that allow you to see through. See through what? Mainly yourself. I get hints of several smiles. But mostly it's Stoneface. Stoneface and I are old buddies. He's one of those old drunk Indian friends who come along every now and then, and you're never really glad to see Old Stoneface. He was not invited, but there he is at the door, he needs to use the telephone, big as life, and he's just this presence that never smiles, never says what he's thinking, never laughs unless it's with the other assembled Stonefaces, which causes you to assume they're laughing at your expense, because they usually are.

I can't recommend the McDonald's in Window Rock. However, they need the money, so feel free to eat there. Just don't expect good service. Expect suspicion. Expect Old Stoneface. Old Stoneface lives wherever Indian culture and white culture intermingle.

Old Stoneface can resist many things. A joke is not one of those things. I tell a joke about Sa, a Navajo deity, to the teenager who serves me the coffee. I only just heard the joke in the parking lot at the sing. I tell the joke in Navajo; it cannot be repeated in a family publication. I get a hearty response. A laugh even. A fire in the eyes.

The coffee is hot. I get a few of those little plastic cups of half-and-half to cool it down. Usually I drink it black. Black and pure. But this time I watch the milky swirl cool my coffee off. That mix of creamer and get-the-cobwebs out. Half cream, half whole milk, half preservative.

I keep wondering what gets preserved, me or the product.

My mother gave me Navajo sings. My dad gave me a particular way of seeing things. I write what I see. Writing is a white people thing. Yet I sing what is there.

The Navajo know this: it's never either-or. It's either *and* or. It's both. It's like white people at a sing. You never really completely understand what's going on. You do not speak the language. You don't belong there. You take photographs and you do not ask permission. What you get, mainly, is ignored. But you do get the taste of it. You swirl to the drum like half-and-half.

Even if what you think you've seen is a powwow.

Funny, the things one learns at McDonald's on a Sunday morning. I take my milky coffee out to my vehicle, where I sip it slowly, watching the yellow arches while I pet my dog. My mom and my dad are in this coffee cup, caught in the middle place between the morbid and the mystical, the musical and the misbehaved. I see them dancing in the swirl contained by Styrofoam. Sipping coffee at McDonald's. I take a photograph of the ritual. I bounce reflections off the windshield. Shadows. Edges. Mongrels. An image for posterity. A fast-food joint. The ordinary. I was there. Another lifetime. Another world.

I seek understanding at a sing, and find it at McDonald's in a cup of coffee.

# 10

# The Blood Runs Like a River Through My Dreams

$M$Y SON IS DEAD. I didn't say my adopted son is dead. He was my son.

My son was a Navajo. He lived six years. Those were the best six years of my life.

The social workers didn't tell me about the fetal alcohol syndrome when they brought my son to the hogan I was living in on the Navajo Nation. Perhaps they didn't know. The diagnosis would come later. As a newborn, Tommy Nothing Fancy looked like any other newborn wrapped in his diaper and his blankies, with his tiny fist in his mouth. Had the Indian social worker said the words "fetal alcohol syndrome," I don't know if I would have done any of it differently.

In the beginning there were no bad things in his head. That would come later. In the beginning he was perfect, even if he was a little small, underweight, and premature. He cried a lot, too. He was perfect to me. I would tie him to his Navajo cradle-board and walk him around, bouncing his growing demons briefly to sleep. We were frequently up all night.

My wife was exhausted.

The doctors at the Indian Health Service said it was nothing. Probably gas.

My solution for coping with the demons of my son was to take them fishing. It worked.

Fishing was this place where I could stand in the middle of the river with Tommy Nothing Fancy strapped to the cradle-board, which I wore on my back. The sun would warm him, and he would sleep. The wind would wake him up, and he would wiggle and kick and giggle and wail with all the voices and singing of the river. He didn't stay tied to the cradleboard very long. As soon as he could walk, he was fishing.

Fishermen will tell you that fishing is about more than catching fish. Fishing with my son was like surrendering myself to the talons of some wondrous beast. Death is always the uncharted logic of its wars, the punished boy child who has been terribly burned, disfigured, standing like an Aztec priest under his father's infinity.

I took Tommy Nothing Fancy fishing everywhere. We fished the lakes of Canada from a canoe. We fished the Colorado, the San Juan, the Rio Grande. We fished in the Sea of Cortés. I will never forget the look on Tommy's face the day I pulled in a bluefin tuna off the coast of Key West. That such a beast could exist was an awesome discovery both frightening and fascinating to my son.

Fishing was our antidote to keep from falling into the blackness Tommy knew was there gnawing at his bones like an animal. A gravity to all his many failures.

When Tommy Nothing Fancy became agitated, he would go outside and sit in Old Big Wanda. Instead of climbing the walls, he would pretend to drive, although he could not see over the steering wheel. I watched the steering wheel go back and forth, sometimes violently. He couldn't hurt Old Big Wanda, and he couldn't take her anywhere, either. I could always immobilize the truck. So I allowed this. He must have driven that old vehicle through a thousand adventures. What he liked best about it was the fact that it was the truck that took us fishing.

We're not really sure when the seizures started, because he could have been having small ones and we didn't know it. The seizures were controlled by medication. For a while.

The demons always came back to turn Tommy Nothing Fancy inside out.

The doctors at the Indian Health Service didn't think it was gas anymore. Now it had a name. They see a lot of fetal alcohol syndrome at the Indian Health Service. You treat the symptoms. There is no cure.

We had a Navajo *hataalii* (medicine man) come to the hogan for sings.

Tommy was surrounded and nurtured by his culture.

My son didn't want to die in a hospital.

He hated hospitals. Hospitals were boring and invasive. People in hospitals were always making him pull his pants down so they could give him shots. My son was very shy.

We did not speak directly of death. Even now, writing about it feels like some amorphous thing come in from the snow and the cold.

For my son, hospitals were analogous to torture.

He kept begging me to save him from the hospitals.

Perhaps he was begging me to save him from death.

I was never very good as a dad. I failed badly. I knew it. Tommy knew it.

I always tried to give him what he wanted. I gave him a stuffed bear once. He called it Poochie. I gave him cowboy boots when he could walk, because I knew he wanted cowboy boots. I gave him toys. I gave him a real fishing rod. Not the cheap, breakable kind of fake kiddie fishing rod you might give a child to pretend with. Fishing was the one place where we did not pretend. We really were fishermen.

I gave him a real Eagle Claw fly-fishing rod. I took him to Canada, where we went brook trout fishing. It was the trip of a lifetime. My son kept fidgeting with his tackle because he wanted it to be perfect. Too many things in a man's life are never perfect; his tackle did not have to be one of them. My son caught a three-pound female brown that fell for a Muddler Minnow in the acid tan waters of the Asheweig River. The rolling hills surrounding the river were lush and green with spruce and tamarack and poplar.

Every man who has a son should give something of himself. This is what the sons are really looking for. I didn't have much, but I had a dog, I had a truck, I had fishing rods. I had upriver treks to Straight Lake Camp, I had pieces of the wilderness, I had Sleeping Spirit Falls, and I had Thunder Bay.

We swam beneath the falls.

At night we cuddled in our sleeping bags and laughed at the dog, who growled when she thought she heard a bear.

It was Tommy's notion that we name the dog Navajo.

I laughed and said okay.

She went back and forth between the two of us like a gentle conduit between his demons and my determination to tame them.

Death, to the Navajo, is like the cold wind that blows across the mesa from the north. We do not speak of it. But I must break with this tradition of silence, because the silence is ill fitting when it comes to FAS, and the fact that so many Indian children have this horrible affliction must be articulated.

This disease is my enemy. A fetus is damaged when the mother drinks alcohol. Any alcohol. It's that simple.

But men drink.

I have listened to many Indian women say this, and they believe it, because it's true.

When pregnant women drink alcohol, there are serious consequences. Our biologics are not the same.

The male body does not nurture fetuses.

But Indian babies do not count. They do not matter. All the old, vicious morality that accompanies the stereotypical image of the inebriated Indian rises to this issue the way a hungry salmon rises to a fly.

There is very little quality to the lives of children who have FAS.

Sometimes none.

I have FAS. Not as badly as Tommy Nothing Fancy had it. My version of the disease manifests itself in some rather severe learning disabilities. All my craziness, my inability to deal with authority, my perceptual malfunctions (I can read entire books upside down), my upside-down imagery, and my rage come from FAS. I have never held a real job for more than a year of my life. Reading and writing are torture for me, so I could understand how they were torture for my son.

I cannot recall my mother ever being completely sober. And there it is.

I am still trying to find ways to forgive her. It's hard. To date, I have mainly failed.

Tribal social-work agencies are overwhelmed with children who have FAS, and there are few Indian people willing to adopt these children.

White people are no longer allowed to adopt Indian children. In their wisdom, the tribes attempt to prevent these adoptions. Yet the number of Indian children who have FAS and who need homes, real homes with real families, is often a daunting challenge for the tribes to keep up with. I knew what I was getting into when I adopted my son. I knew the risks. I knew the possibilities. Life on the reservation was nothing new to me.

When People Who Should Know made the point that fetal alcohol syndrome is a racial epidemic on Indian reservations, they were not exaggerating.

My son kicked holes in the wall once. I have yet to fix the holes.

In many ways he was like the wolves among us.

And he could bite.

The Bureau of Indian Affairs school down the dirt road from my hogan held a Western Dance Night, a fundraiser, which turned into a drunken brawl. Drunk Navajo and beer cans all over the parking lot of an elementary school. These were the parents of the Navajo children who attended the school. It was a bad example for the kids to see. When I talk to my Navajo friends about how such drinking is inappropriate—not in a bar, but in an elementary school—they sincerely, honestly look at me as if they have no idea what I'm talking about.

Old Stoneface lives.

These are people I love. These are *my* people. These are the people my mother came from. These are the people who call themselves the Diné.

So I just pick up the beer cans, and my heart breaks.

Indians are only doing it to themselves.

Remember: it was done to us long before we started doing it to ourselves. Remember.

When you drive through White People Town there's a big sign downtown that encourages Navajo to drink "desert wine."

In moderation, of course.

Not long ago, another Navajo drunk was found underneath this sign, frozen to death in a ditch.

There are varying degrees of FAS. I have seen children with cases so bad their bodies are twisted like pretzels and they are confined to wheelchairs. Many of them are completely nonverbal.

They can't communicate.

They live life in a diaper.

FAS affects individual children differently. There is no way to predict what it will do to you next.

FAS seems to be mainly neurological. With Tommy Nothing Fancy it was manifested in epileptic seizures and out-of-control behavior. He was the terror of schools and teachers and bus drivers and nurses. I thought I could see him getting duller with every seizure. One seizure was so severe they had to put the boy

under general anesthesia. Life under general anesthesia—
asleep—is no life.

The seizures seemed to be eating away at his brain. Watching him get duller and duller was the hardest part of it. There had been a time when this child had an edge as sharp as the edge on a razor.

He was smart.

He was an uppity Indian.

He knew things.

You have them while you can. And then you don't have them anymore.

*Patty-cake, patty-cake, baker's man, roll 'em and roll 'em as fast as you can.*

He knew he was slowly dying, even though we had never discussed it openly in such specific terms. But he knew.

The slowness was killing both of us.

He was forgetting things now. He took a walk down the dirt road and got lost, and I found him in the woods crying. It was dangerous to let him out of my sight.

More seizures led to more trips to the hospital.

"I don't want to be in a hospital," he said.

"Where do you want to be?" I asked.

*Then toss them up in the oven to bake.*

"I want to go fishing," he said.

We are still swimming underneath Sleeping Spirit Falls. The water roaring and tumbling.

The social worker, who always seems very tired, leaves you with this living bundle of blankets, diapers, booties, baby powder, formula, crying, kicking, fists balled up with those tiny fingers. The eyes aren't focused yet—and one never will be—and the first thing you do is inspect the goods.

Naked.

Indian babies are brown and soft, and almost purple when they scream.

Suck that little fist.

Chickenpox was fun.

I didn't know that when the pox comes, it forms horrible little scabs all over your penis. I would bathe him in a bath of water and baking soda. Already the sound of water seemed to soothe him.

If someone had said to me in the beginning, "fetal alcohol syndrome," I can't say I would not have done this. I *would* have done this. I loved him from the moment the social worker brought the bundle to my door. I was his dad.

I never thought of him as adopted. I thought of him as mine.

There were times when I could have sworn I had given birth to the little shit.

Bus drivers hated him. Teachers hated him. Nurses hated him.

His dog loved him. She often slept at the foot of his bed.

I was not good about sharing him. Even with the woman who was my wife at the time.

Now I had a fishing buddy.

The sound of water would stop his crying.

The doctors tell me it was unusual that he lived as long as he did. I know this: Tommy Nothing Fancy lived as long as he did, all the way to the age of six, because I took such good care of him. We were inseparable. I taught him how to fish. But the enthusiasm was completely his.

I still have his tackle box. I cannot open it. Perhaps someday I will.

The stuff inside will be perfect.

. . .

My wife wanted Tommy to die in a hospital. I do not blame her for feeling this way. Institutions like hospitals lend the illusion of control. Americans have turned birth and death into the landscape of the experts. My wife was a modern Indian. She wanted Tommy Nothing Fancy to die surrounded by his family and by a medical community with its own agenda. It was the normal, modern thing to do. Perhaps they could save him. Perhaps not.

Tommy Nothing Fancy wanted to die with his dad and his dog while fishing in the Rio Hondo.

I know because in his own way he told me so.

My wife hated me for telling her this. She begged. She pleaded. She screamed. She pounded the walls.

But the hospitals and the doctors had never made Tommy better. They seemed helpless in the face of the damage that had been done.

Our marriage could not withstand the stress. We are now divorced. I understand the anguish I put her through. But Tommy Nothing Fancy did not want to die in a hospital.

I took my son fishing in the Rio Hondo. Our dog loved to romp around the rocks of the Rio Hondo gorge. She barked at crows.

The place where the Rio Hondo runs free and crystal clear, paradise lost, again, is filled with spectacular brown trout. It is a place where the sun glitters golden on the gravel of the riverbed, and life with all its prowess, its struggle, its tenacity, and its yielding exists in a turbulent crescendo all around you as it rushes downstream, unhindered by the complicated likes of man. I was catching brown trout. I was thinking about cooking them for dinner over our campfire when Tommy Nothing Fancy fell. All that shaking. It was as if a bolt of lightning surged out of control through the damaged brain of my son. It wasn't fair. He was just a little boy who liked to fish. I went to him like I had gone to him a thousand times before. I was holding him when he died. He just stopped breathing. CPR was not effective. The two of us were wet. The dog licked him, barked, and ran in circles. The fish escaped.

Back into the river.

Just the soft sound of the river, with its unruly grandeur and its fluid savvy.

I carried Tommy Nothing Fancy to my truck and put him in the back on a blanket.

We are so alone now.

No more patty-cake.

I made a second trip to retrieve his tackle. I could not leave this perfection behind.

He was so flawed. But his fishing tackle was sublime.

The pediatric neurologist at the hospital had seen FAS deaths before.

"He died fishing," I said.

He had lived fishing, too. I was glad I could give him that. Anyone could have given him hospitals. I was not anyone. I was Tommy Nothing Fancy's father.

We are still swimming under the water at Sleeping Spirit Falls. The water roaring and tumbling. The blood runs like a river through my dreams.

The dog and I drove back to the Navajo Nation that night by ourselves. The shadows of the mountains loomed before us. *Patty-cake, patty-cake, baker's man, roll 'em and roll 'em as fast as you can.* It took me a long, long time before I could cry, and when I did, I thought the universe had ended. First gear is mainly torque. Second gear turns corners. Third gear gets you on the highway. Fourth gear let's you fly. Learning to release him is going to take me some time.

# 11

# And the Dreams Come Down
# Like Thunder in the Rain

*I* HAVE A recurring vision, a nightly dream where my cowboy
fisherman father, the white man whom I look like and take after, returns to me mounted on a horse. Life itself seems suspended. His despair can fill the sky like starving buzzards. Riding dragons. Him struggling against some unseen force, a
monumental void, a fissure in the earth deep below, and the
stars fall in the echoes of the woods.

His compass was a savage thing. I do not want to be pulled

up onto the horse with him. His no-nonsense demeanor always extended itself to me like thunder rumbles softly but distinctly through rain, a darkness lingering on the horizon, but ride with him through the dream I must. I am compelled to make it through what is my own reluctance. I am his son. He is the part of me that has no culture, that has no people, that only has the light, which is a ruthless omnipotence. I reach up, climb aboard, hang on. The animal is a visceral power between my legs. There is no saddle. No stirrups. Nothing to ground us to the horse. We pass fields of weeds and thistles. We are riding through the woods toward the river where I know my father keeps his canoe. I ask him where we are going but he ignores the questions of a boy. The horse snorts, scarfs up the ground, protesting two riders riding him. Trots. Canters. Your life in your teeth.

My father is alive again.

We are going somewhere but I do not know where and I do not know why. All I know is the how of it, and negotiating that takes all of my focus and all of my strength as well.

My father's canoe is almost hidden upside down in the weeds near the shore of a river. I can feel the wind run through these woods and it seems to talk with me.

"Go, go," the wind seems to say. It was a song, too.

"But I am always going," I respond. I am defensive even with the wind.

I wish there was something other than my father to hang on to. But there is nothing. He's it, and I hang on knowing that somewhere along the current of the dream my father will disappear. I do not trust him not to do it.

My father looks at me oddly. "Do you always talk to the wind?" he asks.

If only he knew. I do not share my secrets with this man. He would not approve. I was a major disappointment to him in his life. His exasperation with me remains prevalent in the dream.

He only thinks he knows me. Our separateness has always been his fault. How could he know that I conduct entire conversations, dialogues, with ghosts, trees, dogs, trucks, and rivers. All of this returns to me in dreams, and all of this is demanding.

"Go, go," the river seems to say. I sigh. There is no definitive destination. No plan. No resolution in dialogues with ghosts. I have outlived them all and so I go.

My father goes about the business of turning the canoe over and putting it in the river. He is young and strong and subliminally threatening. He has no idea what to do with a son. He sits in the bow of the canoe and paddles. I do not know what becomes of the horse. It is a dream, and dreams have their own colors and momentum. I can only see my father's back. I sit in the stern which means that steering the canoe is up to me. It's not that I can't do it. It's that I cannot do it exactly to his specifications. He wants it done perfectly but I cannot negotiate the river perfectly. We go with the current from side to side. He won't look at me but just digs in with his paddle, which, like the man who uses it, seems made of wood.

Finally he turns around. "Don't let snakes fall from branches into the canoe," he says. I do not panic but it's there within arm's reach—that panic that it's up to me to learn these lessons he must teach. How I am supposed to prevent the snakes from falling from branches into the canoe is an enigma. None do. But I am prepared to flip them into the river with my paddle. I let something go and learn to endure him and his river, too.

"Go, go," the clouds seem to say. But I am always going and no response is needed. It could definitely rain.

· · ·

We stop and build a campfire in a sand embankment. "Go, go," the river seems to say.

But we will be here for a short time while my father stands in the middle of the river and casts for trout. I sit in the sand and watch. He would like for me to join him and compete. But I refuse. Again, I am a disappointment to him. I am stubborn. I will not compete. He cleans his catch with a hunting knife that glints silver in the setting sun. The blood from the fish drips down the side of a rock onto the ground. My father smiles and says he hopes he has taught me how to never be hungry. I say nothing and wonder if he knows anything at all about the world I live in which is not his world. "Go, go," the sunset seems to say. But I am always going and long to stop.

We pitch a small tent which I sleep in. My father sleeps outside the tent as if to guard me with his knife from cats and bears.

I dream within the dream, and dream of staying right here perhaps forever. "No, no," the snakes in the canoe seem to say. "Go, go." And in the morning we are gone. Our presence was nothing more than a whisper in the evening chill.

I do not know why he brings me to this place of dreams. Only that he does.

We spot a pickup parked alongside the river. His vehicle has been waiting for us. Now for some interminably long ride through these woods, rivers, mountains, plains, corn fields, there is no other traffic. Only us in his vehicle. "Go, go," he seems compelled to say. But what he asks is if I want to stop.

"No, no," I tell him. "Don't stop." Stopping is a sin. I am already enough of a disappointment to this man who takes me to so many different places. The blood from fish has soaked the earth.

Heads. I must bury the fish heads in the sand with my hands. Go, go.

"I'm the one who was a disappointment to you," he says. "I couldn't *make* you grounded."

All the horses ran away.

We pull into the parking lot of a bar. I wonder how he gets away with bringing me into so many bars, but he does. My mother is sitting at a corner table, which is dark. They drink beer and say very little. She asks him for some coins. Her long black hair flows like fish blood down a rock. She dances in the center of the room and entices him to dance with her. The two of them in their cowboy boots and jeans. He dances close to her and she laughs. I chew on ice cubes and eat peanuts that I shell. "It wasn't his fault!" she says to me. "Go, boy, go."

We three climb back into his pickup, which pulls a horse trailer. I am driving and scared to death.

"He's scared," she says.

"He has to learn," my dad explains.

It is night and I cannot see the blacktop.

"Okay, back it up," my dad commands.

I stop the truck. I cannot back it up.

"He has to learn how to back it up," he says.

But I cannot do it with the trailer attached. It is too much to learn. I cannot learn all the things he would have me learn. Go, go.

The cab of the vehicle smells of alcohol, cigarettes, adult things, and I smell something like a dog. My parents laugh again. My jeans are still soaking wet from the river and heavy with the pulling of the journey.

We drive to a cabin in the woods again where my mother makes us eggs. My dad drowns his eggs in ketchup.

I sleep in the loft of the cabin. I climb down in the morning and escape on his horse, which has a saddle now. Through the woods again, and the dreams come down like thunder in the rain. My despair can fill the sky like starving buzzards. Riding dragons. Struggling against some unseen force, a monumental void, a fissure in the earth deep below, and the stars fall in the echoes of the woods. My compass is a savage thing. My own vehicle waits for me in a clearing. Go. Go. Your life in your teeth.

# 12

# On Being Homeless

SHE ARRIVED beaten with her beaten truck out of tune—
mainly, the muffler was missing—and her two little girls who
had been arguing all day as their mom drove. They camped in
a tent on the site next to mine.

America is always on the run.

I heard them before I saw them. I thought they might go
away, hoped they might go away, but when I heard the unmis-
takable sound of tent stakes being driven into the ground, I

knew they had arrived to stay for at least a while. It is an ominous sound. It means steel hitting steel and I'm here.

Driving tent stakes is often hard to do in this part of New Mexico as the ground is primarily rock. But she's mad and pounds away at the tent stakes as if determined not to let what she has—precious little—get blown away. It wouldn't take much of a Navajo wind to destroy everything, including her babies—any good storm could do it—but it wouldn't be because she hadn't tried to protect them. She had protected them fiercely, but the wind would come because it was the wind, and the wind can be depended on to batter you back with its own ferocity, and the wind would ultimately be the victor in this battle that had brought this woman with her children here.

You don't pound tent stakes so furiously like that unless you mean it. They would be my new neighbors now, so I peeked over at them just to see if it could be done without my becoming engaged.

It could not be done. She was a talker.

I recognized the signs. You start exhibiting the symptoms when you've spent too much time with children and you're beginning to crave adult company. You get the little monkey crazies. You begin to see cartoon characters in sane places like the post office. Her name was Maxine. Her truck had Texas plates. She had a thick Texas accent and she was on the run. She believed in demons. "Too many people got too many demons in 'em, all the demons scratching, you know, trying to get out, and sometimes they do, they escape, those mealy slimeballs, they nibble away atcha until there ain't not a thing left in the house to feed 'em. Don't bother looking in the fridge because the demons cleaned it out, too. Demons. I know I got mine."

Such women are always on the run from their husbands. I can always tell. It's the way they look at you with that contradicting mixture of fundamental reason and distrust. They want to like you, but to stop hating you would be like looking straight into the sun — the glare might blind you or at least make you go mad. After all, you're a man. You're one of *them*, the enemy, and there's nothing you can do to hide it.

Her truck was old. Her tent was raggedy (and would prove leaky). Her children had that pale quality as if all they had ever lived on were day-old doughnuts, which was not too far from the truth.

It was not an accident that the campsite she had been assigned was next to mine. There were worse people to live next to. It wasn't like she was going to be playing loud rock late into the night and having wild sex with bikers on the picnic table. Those things did happen here, but even the wild rock bikers wanted to avoid the homeless, those of us who had post office boxes over at the post office and lived quietly over here in our terror and our drabness. We were the untouchables.

I wondered how long it would take for her to borrow something. I gave her a couple of minutes, which turned into a couple of hours, which is about how long it took her to get her children's supper on the picnic table. They were eating hot dogs stuck through with willow sticks but needed mustard. The skinny little wisp whose name was Molly shyly asked if I had any. It was about all I had. It was warm mustard (I was out of ice) but it would do.

The other little girl's name was Ringwald. Now I know beyond the shadow of a doubt that white people have to have their heads examined. This particular little girl was fondly referred to as Ring.

When they were awake they could be loud. The greatest thing about small children is that eventually they sleep.

It rained that first night they camped next to me. The New Mexico wind took out all of Maxine's severely pounded tent stakes. Their tent leaked and they became undone. I have been undone so many times in my life; I stopped counting all the ways years ago. I could see the three of them struggling and crying in the rain. Maxine is swearing up a Texas storm at the clouds who have betrayed her. I get out of my truck to help. Saying nothing where women even in these situations seem to have to talk. We put one child in the cab of Maxine's pickup. We put the other wet kid in the cab of my pickup. I had extra Indian blankets. Both children are hysterical and exhausted. They have all been driving hard to get here. Maxine sits with me in the back of my truck inside the camper shell.

We are the kind of people who can see in the dark like cats. We are our demons.

"Thanks," she says. "Does it rain like this often?"

I do not spare her the truth. "It does."

"Oh great! Just wonderful! What next?"

The most basic reality to being homeless is that you never really know what's coming next. News is not usually good.

The long miles they have traveled together—on the run from what?—only to find their thinness here like living in an old worn-out shoe where the past will dim with the dimmer switch just beyond immediate thoughts and such intangibles as hunger have been condemned. Everything they owned had been soaked.

I was instructed to call her Max. We watched the blackness and the rain together until the sun came up, and then it rained all of the next day, too.

It had come to this.

I am living in a state park in my truck with my dog. Hey, I

blame myself as much as anyone. It is almost winter and the cold is coming. In fact, it already comes at night. The cold is a bitter thing and not sweet in any way.

There are fewer people in the campground now that it's getting cold. All summer, white people have been coming here with their recreational vehicles, their motor homes, their all-terrain vehicles, their dirt bikes, their big camping vans equipped with satellite dishes, their trailers with their shiny trucks. All summer, white people have been coming here with their barbecue grills, their boom boxes, their blue-light bug zappers, their high-tech camping gear, their rock-climbing equipment, the ropes you hope they will hang themselves with, their dogs, their kids who wreck the showers, and their two weeks of desperation off. You notice that they see through their own chaos and around your rocky edges, too. You are decent enough. But you still look homeless. It takes something away from you like some thief has come along and robbed you blind. Beyond the desperation are the other desperations.

You look like just another migrant worker to them—as you would to any normal, nice, working American—and mostly they avoid you with a vaguely suppressed horror that seems to leap from them like some great drowning of rats. Most of these people leave you alone but steal their furtive glances at what you have, taking inventory, even as they construct you for themselves by what you lack. The absence of necessary things defines you staring out at others while you illuminate the interior recesses of the brain with the horror of the sun and the knowledge that there is no such thing as consolation.

You don't have no mojo cell phone.

You got no one to call.

You don't have no mojo TV, and sometimes you wish you could see the news, or get unexpectedly invited in, inside the hushed luxury of the trailer next door where the news is on, which they watch with intelligent, articulated analysis.

Being so smart and smug and all.

They have potato chips, too.

But no. You do not get invited in.

All summer, white people have been coming here bringing insulated facsimiles of the cities and White People Towns where they're from, locking up their trailers airtight at night, the electronic blue light inside their tin compartments flickering as I sit out here at my picnic table (with the cooler) in the dark (writing by flashlight) and wondering what I will do.

About circumstances. About being haunted by the long traces of a life, and hemmed in by the iron fences of my many invincibilities.

People drunk on luck seeking souvenirs come here, too, bringing the plasticity of suburbia with them. "Are you camping here?" they sometimes ask. The brave ones will approach you.

"No," I tell them. "I live here. I'm writing."

People look at me strangely.

But mostly they look away as if they have no eyes or as if their eyes are made of glass.

Maxine works on the engine of her truck, refusing all help from any male, and her children run and play everywhere. She is a feast of oil, grease, and pure frustration.

"I took his tools!" she yells over at me.

Then she laughs. It is a Texas laugh and big.

These are children of the mud, and have been attacked by ticks, and have dragged their balding dolls by the hair through dirt. Anticipating sober triumphs to their business of being girls, and staggering their extraordinary way across the earth which attaches itself to them and under their nails like phosphorus glows ghostlike against the coming dark. Where her children's eyes are a steel gray, Maxine's eyes are veined with red like a Martian landscape and well beyond the ephemeral imitations of fatigue.

Other children — the children of the things — pull away and watch warily.

Those of us who have been assigned to this section of the campground are like something vile that smells. We are something they have stepped into. Something horrid.

Being homeless is like constructing some great hall of mirrors where everything and everyone is distorted. Sometimes I find wood other campers leave behind and I build my cooking fires. I share my cooking fires with Maxine, who is a much better truck mechanic than she is a cook. We two have many things in common, too many things in common, and some unsaid underbelly of the nightmare that is homelessness. Neither one of us knows exactly how it came to this. It all just falls apart one precious piece at a time until all of the pieces are gone and it cannot be held together.

Not with rope. Not with glue. Not with duct tape. And not with sanity either.

I'm not sure I could make a list of the specific reasons. I am not sure that anyone who becomes homeless could. You have left that wholesome place where things like lists are relevant. Or you are apt to list the big events like divorce or death or being fired from a job. But it's the little things that come creeping up on you, the way the cold comes and slips into the meat that is your numby toes. Frostbite is inevitable.

I know this: you wear out your own confidence like the frayed end of one of those ropes the tourists bring. Everything just goes wrong and no amount of planning makes it better. You can pound your tent stakes into the ground as madly and forcefully as you please. The wind will come along and rip them out. I sit here with my pencils and write on yellow legal pads. No computer. No typewriter. Just the barest of essentials. I look at every loss now like my arthritis screams in this cold rain.

Molly informs me that she is a writer too, and sits beside me at this lonely picnic table with her papers and crayons. Someone has taught her how to spell her name, which comes out more like Holly than Molly and she is very pleased.

She asks me questions about Indians and informs me that they have Indians in Texas, but not like the Indians they have here.

The Navajo come here but not to camp. The Navajo come to fill their jugs and containers with water. Many Navajo still do not have water. And so they come to places like this where the water is free and no one harasses them too much as they replenish their water supply from the spigot of an empty camping spot.

Imagine a small yet honest Navajo hogan hidden somewhere nameless and remote. You are surrounded by towering red rocks. There is no running water here. Wells are enormously expensive and have to be drilled very deep, if they can be drilled at all. More and more Navajo are getting connected to more and more infrastructure. Imagine a hogan that supports six to ten people and what water they have is what water they themselves truck in, usually in plastic barrels. The Navajo often bring their dogs with them as they go through the necessary chore of bringing home the water.

My dog lives here with me, and when it gets cold she curls up in her tumble of Indian blankets in the back of the pickup. She avoids the noise of children as she doesn't seem to trust them.

I am still able to buy dog food and Navajo is often generous enough to share it with me so what we have will stretch. She does not blame me for being homeless. I do enough of that for both of us. What we have has to stretch sometimes to the breaking point. Someone I used to know called it "making do." We are making do. And dog food isn't all that bad once you get used to it. I don't think I could stomach cat food, though. I eat the canned dog food very slowly with a fork. As if I'm sitting down to a meal of steak.

Maintaining an illusion by enacting something of a ritual keeps you focused on the ritual versus the fact you are eating dog food. At least you are eating it with a fork. The ritual helps make the stuff go down. I am, of course, insane. Don't let anyone ever tell you that being homeless isn't insane, because it is. Being homeless is the madhouse of the monkey gang. A pouring of oil on the waters in this clutch of hell that burns the air with the smell of flagellating whips. A terrible bargain in the bad market of the losers. Any life that is lived in such a way that other human beings cannot see you — or see right through you — has to be insane. Children who are camping here stare at me as I shave in the public bathroom with the shower. And then they run.

I am the boogieman and might eat them. Knowing so little of hunger, they think I could roast them on a stick, turn them slowly, fat spitting deliciously over my hobo cooking fire. You have to be insane to do this. To surround yourself in these little plots (we all have numbers and dates of departure on our campground cards) with that part of white America that has to get away.

There are other homeless people who live here. They can always tell in the campground's office who we are, and we get relegated to a particular corner of the campground. The only time we really rub shoulders with the tourists is when there's an event like the hot-air balloon festival. The campground fills up early. We homeless love the balloon festival and the big balloons with their wicker baskets, and we wish that we, too, could lift off in some silent yet spectacular goodbye.

Never to be seen or heard from again.

Some time ago I made the decision that I would not just write but that I would live on my writing. I would be brave and simply face it. It was the most insane thing I ever did.

I was on the run but could not fathom what I was on the run from. There were, of course, fools who encouraged me. My friends. People who said they liked my writing. Perhaps because they never took any of these crazy risks themselves. It was easier watching someone like me go down the tubes.

But then few of them know where I am now. I don't want them to know, and if they knew they would wish they didn't know. I am deeply humiliated by my homelessness, but there it is.

I am ashamed of what I have done with the gift that was my life. It runs fluidly through my fingers and pours itself on the ground at my feet. It was a life once. It did things. It had value. Now I do not want to see or be seen by anyone I used to know. I don't have to worry about it too much, though, because I don't look like my former self—my health is draining away like liquid I cannot contain in my fingers. I stare every morning into the metal thing the state park calls a bathroom mirror and wonder who the dead man is. Every two weeks I move to another campground not unlike this one. Two weeks go by, and then I move back again. The dog isn't particular about where we camp. She seems to be my only friend. However, I am particular about where we camp. I like shade.

. . .

I am getting used to the musical sound of Maxine's children.

Maxine follows me when I move to the other campground. More pounding of the tent stakes. The picnic tables are not so nice here, but there is a lake and her girls swim in it. Nothing but nothing washes off the dirt.

"I tried scrubbing them with scrub brushes," Maxine explains. "But all it did was grind the dirt in deeper. Soap's expensive but those tourists leave plenty of it behind in the showers." I could always hear Maxine and her wisps next door in the women's showers as Molly and Ringwald ran around starkers in their flipflops.

Somehow they became attached to me the way the dirt had become attached to Maxine's girls.

It was nothing I ever thought I would write about because there was no real drama to it. Or any drama I could see.

I have learned many things about writing since I started living like this on the edge. Off the edge. Over the edge. On into the free fall of the monkey gang. Still, I know nothing about the technical stuff of writing or where to put a comma. What I know about writing goes beyond where to put your commas. What I know about writing has to do with where you put your heart.

Maxine's little girls bug me but get easily bored. I sit at a picnic table all day writing and they think it's very weird.

I have sold a lot of junk lately. Pornography, which is not immune to rules and is enormously depressing to write. So I stopped writing it. Now I write Chamber of Commerce advertising copy. Anything not too painful that might pay my way. Dog food is not expensive. Less than a buck a can. I keep my post office box at the state park, but have no immediate way people can reach me, and find that white editors do most of their business over the phone, which means they get real frustrated dealing with me. I get frantic notes from them stating that I forgot to give them my phone number. I did not forget. They send me overnight mail, which I find vastly wasteful. When things get really bad I just send them my bills.

The bills do not get paid.

I declare bankruptcy. When I tell the judge what it is I do for a living he shakes his head. And then it's over.

The story that pursues me and eludes me is about the Navajo. I am writing about what the uranium mines have done to the Navajo and find that it is a story both mysterious and compelling. No one has really told this story and no one wants to publish it either. The Navajo are like the homeless. Let them eat their bones.

Maxine comes over with something hot and sweet and chocolatey to drink.

I am not afraid to read her some of my work, which she asks to hear.

"I write country music myself, you know," she says. "The lyrics and the music." Someday she would sell something.

Her little girls play with Navajo children who come here to collect the family water. Other white children will not play with them, and laugh when they see those balding dolls.

Race is still the Great American Dilemma like some necessary breath has been squeezed and strangulated from your very throat. There is no escape from it, just as you know that luck is really ruthlessness. Max and I agree that all writing is political. It doesn't matter where you live. You are writing either about the status quo or about a change in the status quo. The stranger comes to town or you take a trip. The story of the stranger who comes to town is the story of a change in the status quo. So is the story about taking a trip.

I take Maxine and her wisps into White People Town so I can show them the library. Molly and Ringwald check out a small mountain of books.

Even as you do research in the dust of libraries you realize that some of the most brutal people in history regularly attended the opera and collected art. I spend hours and hours in the library stacks and unexpectedly come across an old collection of telegrams between the War Department in the West and the government in Washington, D.C. People in government were talking about a plot to kill Sitting Bull years before Sitting Bull was murdered.

The telegrams are so old they almost dissolve into dust just touching them. No one has seen them in well over a hundred years. You discover things when you're homeless. Like shortcuts through fields of sage and trash.

The way to shut us up — to denigrate and destroy the truth we hear and see — is to render us unworthy and unsuccessful and without homes or roots.

The homeless are insane.

I spend my evenings reading by flashlight in a sleeping bag with the dog, who fortunately is still dog enough to love me more than any other thing.

I stand in the small post office and take my time reading my mail. Mail is a link to another world. It is not, however, a world that I fathom in any way. Most of my mail is from editors who tell me they have no idea what it is I am attempting to do. Some of them go so far as to demand some kind of explanation. But I have no explanation. If I knew exactly what I was doing I have no doubt I would not be doing it.

My work often attempts to take the dynamics of the mythology I have learned and put it into a modern context because I am of the belief that nothing ever really changes. But I am told, by learned folks who ought to know, that it cannot be done.

I am sitting with the dog in the back of the truck watching and listening to the rain come down. Everyone except us homeless folks has packed up and left. The rain seems to spoil their fun. The rain pounds against the truck as if to beat some flimsy tin drum.

Maxine knocks. She climbs in the back. "Rain again," she says.

"I would like to hear you sing something you have written," I tell her.

She does not bother to go back to her truck for her guitar but starts singing with no musical accompaniment. I recognize the voice immediately. Maxine writes her songs for revenge.

I do that too, but my revenge is writing.

"The girls are reading in the tent," she says. The tent is always being reconstructed. "I hope it doesn't get blown away again like that first night we got here." She can laugh about it now.

I read to her a part of the novel I am writing about Navajo children who are exposed to the dangers of an abandoned uranium mine.

"You mean they never fixed these places up?" she asks. She is not surprised.

"No, they just left them, and sometimes they left them leaking poison into the drinking water of the Navajo, which is why you see so many Indians collecting their water at the state park."

Max nods. "It's like a real book, all this writing on these yellow pads you do."

I did hope so some.

"Let me sing you this story I made up in Texas. It's about these two people I used to know."

One of those people was, of course, her husband.

Maxine and I could have filled all the pages of all the libraries with the names of people we used to know. Now none of them know where to find us.

Maxine is hired to sing in a white people bar.

I babysit the girls in my truck without even thinking about how odd it is we live in trucks.

The girls brush and comb their dolls' hair. Brush and comb. Brush and comb.

What hair these dolls have left.

One day I receive an unexpected payment for an article I had totally forgot having written. I go into White People Town and buy two new dolls at a toy store in the mall. The new dolls have hair.

Brush and comb. Brush and comb. Run off into the sunset in your flipflops.

Maxine came back one night with a white people newspaper. There was a job advertised in there for a local reporter.

There wouldn't be any of the big stories I wanted to write about. It would all be little stories.

"The little stories *are* the big stories," Maxine said. "Every now and then everyone needs to come in out of the rain."

I would apply. I would get that job, too.

The little girls do not yet know they have no home — no bedroom from which to watch the Texas moon — but seem intent on living out their grand adventure where at least for them every livid moment is the very first electrifying instant of eternity.

They play princess as aptly as they play ballerina and usually act out these delicious fantasies fully decked in ballerina costume (Princess wears a crown from Burger King). The cold weather means that now they have to wear their Salvation Army winter coats as well, but they do not allow these extra clothes to break the illusions that compel them as they dance around the red rocks, the dumpsters, and the asphalt road that circumnavigates the campground.

Maxine's husband found them, of course. He arrives in a car with the back seat full of laundry. She would end up doing the wash in the white people laundromat in White People Town. Another of her demons had clawed its way out and you could see the blood swimming in her eyes. He had been sick with grief as many such men are commonly sick with the grief that eats them from the inside out because that's what demons do. It's often just a question of whose demons are the dominant demons, and who backs down, not in the face of failure like falling off a cliff, but more like a slow grinding away at the bones until you have been infinitely pulverized. He wanted his family back.

I was the homeless guy who lived next to them in his truck with his dog. I wasn't family.

Only sort of.

This tall, brooding man did not seem to be a monster. In fact, he looked ordinary and rather sad.

Maxine seemed a little relieved. It was beginning to snow now and the snow could come in spits and gusts. The dog and I would buy more Indian blankets at Wal-Mart to keep warm. I kept writing. My hands would swell up from a horrible and excruciating arthritis. My pencils were my bones.

They pulled up tent stakes. They packed their dolls. I got kisses and suddenly realized that homelessness is this place where you hardly ever get kisses. Kisses from two scrubby Texas urchins. It would have to do.

I do not know why I wept when they left, but I did. We weren't even family. I was all alone at the state park now. Even the snakes had disappeared into the ground. Even the snakes had more of a sense of place than I did. If it hadn't been for the dog I would have given up.

But I did not give up. I got that job as a reporter for the white people paper. I wrote the local fishing report. I was set to cover high school sports. At night when no one else was around I borrowed the paper's one and only typewriter and turned my many notes on legal pads into a novel. It was a success of sorts, putting it all down like that. Being able to write a novel at all is not unlike the way you tend to children as you put them down because they are beyond exhausted and can go no further with the long traces of their lives but are hemmed in by that thing we call at long last sleep.

Homelessness is the underbelly of America. I was there. I was there when another person with her homeless children found some passing refuge in what small things I had to give, some dry place out of the rain, and they in turn gave back to me and allowed me to brush and comb those pitiful dolls' hair, as if the dolls were queens, because they were to the girls. There is no escape from being defined by what you lack. It follows you everywhere. A small package arrived at the paper one day addressed to me. It was a tape. I knew who it was from.

Maxine must have found some rest from the demons that drove her. There's about an hour of singing there and accompaniment on guitar. The songs are like the rain and the power of the words is enough to rip stakes from the ground. You will be soaked with it, too. Many of the songs are about loss, but behind the words are haunting melodies that take you other places. I no longer look at every loss like my arthritis screams in this cold rain, but now know all my losses for illuminating events (hard as they might be) that light the brain with the horror of the sun and the knowledge that there is no such thing as consolation.

# 13

# Michif's Tape

*I*WAS LIVING in the Big Wild West and working in a suburban high school. It was a normal school for normal kids run by adults who cranked out normalcy as if it were a chain-link fence factory, and here we were cranking it out and cranking it out, all the fine little links, miles and miles of normalcy dividing and protecting us from deviance of any kind. Such institutions are everywhere in America. They are so ordinary we don't think about them but remain content to let them hum and buzz along of their own volition. They come with vast parking lots that seem to stretch the asphalt out to the horizon of the desert becoming asphalt deserts of their own.

It has been suggested that such goliaths — the physical layout was as sprawling as it was daunting — don't work very well, but like all institutions this particular school's main purpose was its own continued existence. Having lived the life I've lived, I distrust most institutions. If you were a student there, your challenge would be to find your niche, but that was true for the adults who worked there as well.

It was just a job. It was not an important job. It would pay the rent. But I really didn't know what it was they wanted me to do. The job description I had been given had been kept purposefully ambiguous.

I didn't care. What I cared about was being able to support myself so I could continue to do the kind of writing I wanted to do.

I had this awful fantasy of becoming a novelist. I had this Big Wild West illusion that after school I could come home to write.

The reality, of course, is that at the end of the day I would be too exhausted and wrung out to write anything. But then the writing life is a flimsy ship and often sinks.

I was not a certified teacher, yet I had a classroom. The fact that you're not a teacher yet you have a classroom means they're going to send you all the children who are giving them problems. I didn't have the word "detention" written on my classroom door. But that would probably come. What was amusing about this setup was that I had no desks. It was just a room. There was nothing for anyone to sit on.

I reported to the assistant principal, who was not a bad guy even if he was severely harassed.

In such settings it's always about the numbers. There were

three thousand students at this high school. It was a big, modern, imposing, impersonal setting, and if you were ever alone in it, the place seemed to echo with a subliminal murmur of its own. It was a shiny, rambling, brick-and-glass sort of place and state of the art as far as high schools go. Everyone had access to a computer and technology. You could get lost there, and I did once. There was a lot of noise and pandemonium in the halls between classes when the kids were around, but you had to wonder if anyone really knew anyone.

The first day of school the assistant principal called me into his office. "I want the two of us to take a walking tour of the student parking lot," he said. "Let's start looking in cars for guns."

The assistant principal was probably fifty. Provoking armed high school students did not seem to be his favorite thing to do and even now elicited a weariness you could hear in his voice.

"Guns?" I was surprised. I thought I would be working with kids. I didn't see myself as the authority figure who walked around in search of guns.

But it was the first day of school and my first day on the job. So I dutifully went with the assistant principal outside to the student parking lot and the two of us walked around looking in cars for guns.

I kept thinking we wouldn't find any guns. But we did. We found hunting rifles in back seats. We found them in trucks.

It was perplexing because you had to be either incredibly stupid or incredibly arrogant to keep a gun in plain view. I was the one, of course, who was incredibly naïve not to know (or remember) that adolescents can be both.

I hated looking for guns and didn't really want to find any. The assistant principal explained that this was something we would do every day.

He also explained that there would be parents who would defend their children's right to bring guns to school. I was incredulous. Incredulous or not, it was true. You really had to wonder if this was education or a giant day-care facility that existed simply to accommodate parents.

I needed the job but I didn't see myself as the gun police. It didn't fit. Walking around the student parking lot made me feel extremely uncomfortable. Finding guns made me even more uncomfortable.

This should have been a job for law enforcement. But no.

I wanted to work with kids. I was good at it. I had done it before. But looking for firearms was not working with kids. If a high school student is bringing guns to school, it's a little late in the day to attempt to reach him by reading off a litany of school rules. Tacking up the Ten Commandments on the wall was missing the forest for the trees. Bringing a gun to school was not a good idea. It was a good way to get attention, though. Attention would be paid. The guns were confiscated.

Students were bringing guns to sports events, dances, and school club activities. When you sat down to talk with these kids they almost always seemed to be threatened by something bigger than they were, something they could not define. And their right to bear arms (they had all the rhetoric) could not be interfered with or abridged in any way.

Well, it could be interfered with. Their right to bear arms was indeed interfered with. But I kept thinking that if a kid was bringing a powerful rifle to school because he (they were always male) thought he had to have it to defend himself, then the message that school was a safe place was a little late in reaching this kid.

Obviously, many of the students did not think school was particularly safe at all. Kids knew but adults seemed to have to have the actual gun in their faces before they could admit that something about the school and the educational system built around the school wasn't working.

"This isn't working," I would mutter to myself as I walked the parking lots in search of guns.

I wanted to work with kids before it became too late. I didn't want to be just another meaningless authority figure consigned to the moral sidelines where all of us functioned in a tragic complexity of blindness. I didn't want to be the jerk who read the riot act. I wanted to reach kids before they brought a gun to school. But my opinions were minority opinions, and playing "gotcha" with teenage males was more concrete than my own ill-defined ways of reaching them with the message that they, too, were involved and responsible for the environment they lived and learned in.

This was high school, not day care. Yet it was the psychology of day care that prevailed in an atmosphere where school was just a place where kids went so parents could hold down the real jobs.

So what if your son brings a gun to school? Perhaps he only did it as a joke. The excuses could get real thick.

We started suspending students on day two. The outcry on the part of the parents was always visceral.

Every day I walked around the parking lot looking for guns. I grew heavier and heavier with the weight of it. Finally I quit. I couldn't confiscate another gun.

"You burned out faster than even I thought you would. I thought maybe you might make it all the way to Christmas," Sondra Sanchez said. Sondra was my friend, a social worker, and she had seen the dark side of it many times. Sondra was a Taos Pueblo Indian but she didn't live in Taos anymore. Now she worked with kids in gangs and children euphemistically called "at risk," and when it was worth the effort, she attempted to salvage one of them.

You salvage them one kid at a time.

There is no other way.

There is no single program that works for everyone. You play an awful lot of it by ear.

You gamble, too. It is always a roll of the dice and time and resources, and sometimes you hold your breath in anticipation that what you're doing will pay off. Working with children is more risky than writing books.

"I keep waiting for some kid to get killed over there, you know, and I can tell you what the fight will be about."

I had always known that Sondra's abilities were amazing, but I never realized she'd be able to read the future.

"What fight?" I asked.

"Oh, someday there will be a fight between two males over a parking space and one of them will have a gun. It'll get ugly, and then it'll make the paper, and we'll all sit around wringing our hands, wondering where we all went wrong. If it gets ugly enough it'll get on TV, but we'll still do all the hand-wringing we always do when we try to figure out these kids. Some kids can't be reached. It's too late, or it's too sad, or it costs too much."

I felt the abstract need to defend my courage, or perhaps it was my sense of masculinity, or perhaps it was both. "I'm not afraid of getting shot," I claimed.

"You should be," Sondra said.

Sondra Sanchez asks me about my writing because she knows about little pieces of the struggle. But I didn't know anyone who could work all day with children and then come home to really crank it out.

I was coming home too numb to write anything.

I find myself shaking my head without even realizing it.

Writing had left me stripped of everything, like an ancient gravestone loses its etched inscriptions of dates and names to decades of rain and snow. It happens one molecule at a time where the solid seems impervious.

Writing was this place where it was impossible to measure just how far down you really were, and the words you struggled to put on paper were nothing more than faint rustlings of wings, more the mosquito than the hawk. Writing was this endless pecking and clucking of the great machine whose only word was no.

I pick my words with Sondra Sanchez carefully. "What really scares me is that I'm wasting my time in a place where there's three thousand kids and how do you reach anyone with those kind of numbers?"

"So you quit?"

"I quit. I want to work with kids. I don't want to play police. It's worse than playing mom or dad, when in fact I can't be any of those things I'm not. It's bad enough when those of us who work in schools have to be pseudoparents, or somehow assume that role, but when we have to be the police, too, it's a lot of straws on the camel's back."

"Still looking for a challenge?" She almost grinned.

I had to chew on it for a minute. Sondra Sanchez was not the kind of woman who asked metaphorical questions. I knew she kept a lot of kids in her bag of challenges.

"What kind of challenge?" I asked.

"I've got this kid on my caseload I'd like you to meet. Everyone involved with him has either washed their hands of him or are about to. His name is Michif and he's half Taos Pueblo Indian and half Apache. This kid is really bad and no one wants him. He's in a foster home right now and they're having a real hard time handling him. He's been institutionalized at Children's Psychiatric in Albuquerque and in and out of the court system all his life. Both parents are dead now. Murdered. We think over a drug deal. Michif is thirteen. He's failed school and the school wants to kick him out. But kick him out to where? This kid is on the fast track to prison and maybe I'm just kidding myself but I keep thinking that the right person might just reach him."

"Why me?"

"You're available and you're usually too dumb to say no. And I want to try just one more time before I give up on him. You don't have to do it — we might be able to arrange some funding out of alternative education's budget, although it would be pretty bare bones. Sondra shrugs. "You could always go back to looking for guns in parking lots."

I could not go back to looking for guns in parking lots.

We arranged for Sondra to bring him to my house. I would talk to Michif and see if I thought there was any hope for it.

I really didn't know what to expect. I knew I would have to rely on gut instinct, which is where most kids like Michif lived.

This kid was about to be put away. I believe that some kids should be put away. But not the ones who can be saved.

If an adolescent can't handle the impersonality endemic to our notion of what modern education is about, that adolescent renders himself or herself disposable. So Sondra Sanchez would bring him over. I wanted to see if he could handle a social situation. The plan was that if I wanted to work with this kid—if I thought it could be done—he would be excused from formal school and work with me one on one. The goal was to get Michif back into school the following year.

I would have one year. No more. I could basically design my own program because everything else had failed.

It would be a huge, untried experiment, but then so was everything I had ever written.

I was expected to fail, too.

I would have access to all the school system's libraries, computers, books, tapes, and just about anything else I needed. But first you have to get the kid through the door.

It is not as easy as it sounds. This particular kid was dug in hard and deep.

I was not prepared for the physical beauty. There is no other way to describe it. He was about as tall as I was, but very slight and very, very dark. And hides behind that shock of hair. Usually you would describe such males as handsome. But he's at that still soft stage where you're not sure if it's a boy or a girl just yet — the Indian hair hides his vulnerability. The skin is smooth, flawless like the skin of a golden girl, but he flutters, too, like only boys flutter in their butterfly leanness while his obvious despondency has the conscience of a stone, and so you know it for the boy it is.

I do not remember what we said. What we said is not important. Time and place are not important here either. I see him standing there alone, swaying slightly like some faint strand of a spider's web, his too large hands plunged into his pockets, fragile, tenuous, aloof in the disdainful way he stared as if the dust itself had saturated all the air. He doesn't say much. He nods, though. He is sitting on the sofa now, in no way dumb, but blunders along the unfamiliar curves, dragging his nothingness through the sunlight and the stones, folding his too long arms and his too long legs, gently swinging his too big feet like fish boats bob about at sea.

He is another frigid season's empty storms and colored swirls and rage where neither poise nor resolve will save him from the fire or the night. He is bewildered, but far too cautious to show much of it, and I imagine he has bled on all the walls, has crawled down roads of mud, and seeing down, down into the deep and wounded spaces now he merely glides across the strange machines and ways of man. He skims along the surface of things, his feet never really touching bottom, and his dark eyelids with their heavy lashes have to weigh five pounds each. How many disembodied curses has he launched upon the world, poor stupid animal, gnarling his words as if he were a prophet searching the meadows and hollows of the earth for something as banal as a home.

He nods. He acts polite. But what I saw were eyes that had retreated to conversations where he listened only to the desert and the dead. Such melancholy happens easily with boys. Girls are more resilient.

"I would have to make it up as I go along. Can you live with that?" I asked.

I had learned many years ago to watch the body and the eyes.

Creativity is often a surprise and often to the person that it's coming from.

The body relaxes for just a bit. The eyes look up. We connect.

If the eyes had remained glued to the carpet we would not have gone to any of the places we went. He was put together but not really composed. And he was full of questions. I could see that. I could feel it in my bones. I knew then and there that this was a kid fighting the good fight. It was the battle of acquiring language. I had been there myself. In many ways I am still there. The prospect of having a teacher for a year who was going to have to make it up as he went along sounded like less structure than this kid was used to having to deal with. Such kids pounce like predators on their lesser prey. But this kid did not make the mistake of underestimating me, and he laughed. The fact that he laughed was a good, good sign. The two of us would now engage in battle. It didn't take this kid long to figure out that he was going to be dealing with more structure, not less, because my attention could be devoted to all his many dilemmas, and I would in all likelihood ride him through his veins before the year was out.

Now I was a teacher.

I had no classroom. I had no parking lot. I had no desks. All I had was a sense of determination that it could be done with such a kid. All I had were the dice. We wash our hands of far, far too many of them without bothering to know them for who they are.

It's fashionable to critique education as having failed, but I can't do that here. I consulted all my education books but I had to throw them out. None of them were going to help me with Michif. I had never been absolutely confident about who was supposed to shoot whom or over what, but knew the sound everyone would make screaming witness over education as if it were a sinking ship. There are many, many dedicated, committed, bright, selfless, tireless, dynamic people who work in education, and it is not my place or my purpose to critique anything they do. All I could do was take one kid and attempt to mold some of his skills so that he didn't completely shut down. Completely shutting down was the real issue here. It's almost impossible to reach them after that.

I have all these wild, untried ideas, theories about working with kids who have failed, how to tap down, down into the thinning shadows of the self, but I know I live in a practical place where what's often best is just to shut up and at least pretend to listen. Working with this kid would be like writing, and on the face of it impossible because everyone says so in a repeated litany unreeled like a film that pretends to say what has never been said.

We would have an awful lot of work to do, Michif and I.

The first thing I went for was his choice of words. His vocabulary was limited and just about every other word was a curse word. Shit, fuck, asshole, et cetera. Language peppered with such frequent obscenities was one of the things that had landed him in trouble with teachers, judges, social workers, psychiatric nurses, and anyone else who wielded authority over him. He had recently told a judge to suck his Indian dick. This was a judge who could have put him in a juvenile detention facility for a long time. But all the juvenile detention facilities were overcrowded and what Michif got was me.

The trick was to recognize it for the insecurity it was and not to mistake it for language — it was more a repertoire of verbal gymnastics designed to put you off in such a way that you didn't demand real language from him.

It didn't take long to shape his language because the capacity for it had always been there. It's a passive sort of racism that unconsciously equates failure with the darker color of the kid. It's a passive sort of racism that trains these kids to pass the state's standardized tests as it assumes that really teaching them the fundamentals of anything is more than they can do. This child's capacity for language had never been tapped into because no one had ever demanded it from the boy.

But I had power because I took it.

Michif was normal in so many ways, and all the good things

in his little life, like his access to fast food, malls, movies, clothes, and everything else he wanted, got scrutinized and controlled by the unrelenting likes of me.

The first thing you have to do is find out what the kid loves and then you have to work with it. Discovering what someone so guarded loves is not easy. He will tell you he doesn't know, and you have to be able to see the truth in it. He *doesn't* know. What he knows is usually buried somewhere in a sea of extraordinary anxiety.

This kid loved McDonald's. He hardly ever got to eat there. So I would take him to McDonald's and make him sit there while I ate all the things he loved while he watched. He would get nothing from me until he made an attempt to change the formidable nature of his language. "Can't I have at least something?" he complained.

It was one of the first times he hadn't told me to stick my head up his ass. The language choices he was used to making weren't working here. I had him right where I wanted him. I gave him one french fry.

It pained me to do it. My success that day was that Michif ate the french fry (silently) instead of throwing it at me. This was progress.

When he finally got to the point where he could conduct an entire conversation with me and not use the word "fuck" once, I took him to McDonald's and allowed him to order his own lunch.

This precipitated a crisis. I knew it would.

"No," he pleaded. "You have to order it for me. I can't."

First there was the issue of having to read a menu. Then there was the issue of money. I would give him the money and he would have to come back with the correct change. This challenge brought much anguish, tears, and bargaining (with no swearing). I wouldn't help him. I would stand behind him while he ordered. But I wouldn't order for him. Institutions protect these kids by taking choices away from them, and children like Michif find something as simple as ordering lunch to be inordinately complicated. It took Michif two months of practice and encouragement (tons and tons of encouragement) before he could order an entire lunch at McDonald's. He would sit in my truck and weep. Finally, he did it. It was a moment of success we savored in silence. Then he handed me a french fry.

"Thanks," he said. "I didn't do too badly, did I?"

The food was right. The change was right. It had taken some reading, some math, some communicative language, some social stuff, and courage, too.

I took the french fry. I popped it in my mouth. I smiled. "You did okay," I said. That one french fry would come to signify an awful lot to us.

Then there was the time I made him make macaroni and cheese. He had to follow the directions on the box. We did not eat that disaster.

We went to museums. We went to art galleries where I got to show him the work of Georgia O'Keeffe. I wanted him to see where she had lived, so I took him to the Ghost Ranch near Abiquiu. It was a two-day trip.

We stay at a motel together. "Aren't you going to jump my bones?" Michif says in the dark.

"Not this trip," I say. "I'm too tired to jump anyone's bones."

He laughs and laughs.

He badly needs an adult in his life who can make light of his mortal situations, his vulnerabilities, without ripping him off and robbing him of the things that make him just a boy.

A trip to actually see where Georgia O'Keeffe painted has to be a far, far better thing than viewing a bunch of slides.

I took him to visit a sculptor who let him work with clay. "It's different feeling it," he said.

We went to the state capitol and watched the legislature in action. We drove to the Grand Canyon where I made him read books on geology. We read the road signs out loud. When he refuses to read a sign I pull the truck over to the side of the road and we sit right there until he tries. He gets very frustrated with me. We went to the Department of Motor Vehicles where I got him a copy of the driving booklet and the test.

His dream was to drive someday, and he was outraged to realize that in order to pass the driving test you had to know how to read.

It wasn't fair. He got all pouty about it.

I took him to the movies. We were watching a film once when he turned around and told a bunch of older, rowdy kids to shut the fuck up or he was going to beat the shit out of them.

These kids turned out to be members of a gang.

His judgment was a little faulty. I had to usher him out of there before he got himself (and me) murdered.

Sometimes you have to protect them from themselves.

This was a kid who had almost no social skills. Nada. He was in many ways a wanderer in a broken cosmos where time, to such a boy, is experienced not by its abstract relationship to the past but by his own immersion in the moment.

Michif wanted to be a Navy SEAL and be trained in the mechanisms of killing people. In his dreams.

I took him to a bigger town that had a Navy recruitment office, and a naval officer explained to him that it all came with an ability to read.

That, too. Ah, his hopes were dashed.

Such kids cannot live too long within the context of a fantasy.

This boy was convinced that kids his own age were out to get him. Really get him. "They're gonna beat me up," he'd say. These were almost always children he didn't know. They could be simply walking down the street but he was convinced they were all out to get him.

He was insistent about always locking every door.

I ignore tons and tons of his beleaguered stuff.

He plays an incredible game of chess. I can never beat him. It is impossible. He knows all the moves and is calculating. We play chess for hours. He takes each game very seriously.

Toward the end of the year he is reading maps. He has me drive to some secret destination—he refuses to tell me where we're going. Since he has done so well, I'm game. Our destination turns out to be the abandoned site of an ancient Anasazi village, and we walk around the place carefully. He points to an area that should contain pots. "Because," he says, "that's where the dump would be."—at least as he envisions how the village was laid out.

He's right. The pots are where he says they should be. We are careful to disturb nothing.

I see this as progress, too, because I know such rage and emptiness lend themselves to vandalism. The pot hunters and petroglyph defacers are people disconnected from any culture, as are the folks who leave their trash behind. But not this time. And not with this boy.

I am beginning to feel that our work together has had an effect. I don't need a standardized test. I also know him for what he doesn't do. He doesn't do graffiti.

In fact, he has a low opinion of it now.

"It isn't art," he claims. "Not like those O'Keeffe paintings we saw are art, you know."

I nod. I say nothing. Yet I know for a fact that one of the judges he was once hauled before had not been amused with what he had once done to a wall with a can of paint.

I am perhaps even more amused that he has an opinion on art at all.

I do not want to wait until the next school year to put this boy back into a classroom setting. Why wait if it's not necessary? I make it my mission to find administrators and teachers who might help. We walk around a junior high. There are no other children. Then we try it when there are kids around. I can see he's terrified, but he also knows by now that he has more support than most. Teachers and administrators and social workers and foster parents and judges have all pitched in and everyone here understands that the battle is never really over. But he has not shut down. That's what we're really doing here. It's something. And he hasn't been in trouble for a year.

One of his ongoing projects has been to keep a diary on tape. At first I had to make him do it, but then he took off with it on his own. I was always so busy planning what we'd do next that I never bothered to tap into his taped diary. It was one of the few things I did not make him write down. I knew that someday I would listen to it (I am not afraid of violating his privacy because I see the diary as a tool to evaluate his progress, and he knows that someday I will listen to it), and when I finally find the time to pop it in the tape machine, I am amazed.

It begins with a long barrage of rage, much of it directed toward me. Then the rage gets tossed around what he calls the other assholes in his life. But as the tape wears on the rage seems to settle some. It begins to get displaced by observations. Some of the observations are insane (like the one about how all the girls want him). Some of the observations are correct (like the one about how people don't like it when you swear). Music that he likes is spliced between observations. Some of it is rock. Some of it is Indian music he has found at the public library. It adds a haunting element to the tape. But it is the inclusion of stories that confounds me.

They are like gems. These are Indian stories, stories of super-natural kids his age who accomplish glorious things. I never knew he could tell such stories. Or that he even had the skills. But there they are. And I am enthralled to discover them, stum-bling as is my way.

The strength of his stories reflects his own inner strength. One hears the beginning of a voice and it shakes me a little bit. I know that if you combine all the voices of all the Indians, you would have stories and storytellers that white people would nei-ther recognize nor care about in any way. White people regard much of what Indians create as primitive, and Michif's stories would be consigned to this category. I know that finding that voice and strength is one thing, but holding on to it is another struggle altogether. I wonder at what I have done. I know I have opened up something enigmatic to him that will prove to be ei-ther a thing of pain or a source of reemergence. It is too early to say.

I have tried to shape things for him so that he can fit into the context of the world—a world that I recognize would destroy him if it could. Perhaps his paranoia was simply more overt than anything I wanted to deal with. His small stab here at what is art would remain obscure to teachers trained in West-ern, white educational methods. What he has done would get relegated to some folklore ideology, when in fact what he is telling is the story of himself. This is where I could kick myself, for he has gone too far by producing something perhaps as beautiful as he is. Ah, the primitive Indian ethos.

His work on his diary—his thoughts, his impressions, his recorded observations, his music, and his stories—always came last, toward the end of the day when everything else had been attended to. Had I known the tensions that he rode, my tendency would have been to make this work first because this is where everything else I wanted could have come from. But again I kept it last—something to be tended to only if there was time—thinking he, too, had to stumble about with the rest of us in the dark to affirm the validity of his experience as his material.

He came to me defined as the murderous, shameful savage who didn't do what he was supposed to do. He leaves me with a tape of stories that are spellbinding in and of themselves. I know this: Michif will never be regimented into anything mindless he is expected to emulate. That is exactly the sort of authority he rejects. The authority he respects is the kind that comes from those internal places that connect.

"This is some of the best stuff I've ever listened to," I tell him.

We are connecting now. It is a place of equals.

"Why don't you share some of your stories with me," he says. "You never do."

"I can't. I wouldn't know how."

"Not even a french fry," he says. "You can do better than that."

So I have to haul them out. All the manuscripts I have put away.

All my many failures.

Here the two of us are wanderers in a cosmos where time is experienced not by its relationship to any sort of cultural past but by our shared immersions in the moment.

"Why do I have to learn this stuff, why is it important to anything?" he would say. If I heard it once I heard it a thousand times. I always had a glib answer.

But here was a talent much bigger than mine. And I have no ready answers for him. All I have is the suggestion of turmoil and sometimes fleeting victory.

The dice I have been holding in my hand have begun to burn my flesh. It is time to roll them.

The big day arrives. He has had his hair cut. He has new clothes. He does not want me to tell him that he will drive all the junior high school girls crazy, but I tell him anyway. I tease. It's good for him and disabuses him of the notion that he is someone who must be taken so seriously. He seems hypnotized (or frozen) by the noise of girls with their friends, not realizing that his days from this point forward will be filled with the noise of girls and their friends. He knows them now about as well as he ever will, which is to say not at all. He closes his eyes and has to psych himself up for this.

It is the first day of real school in a new school year. Michif does everything he can not to tremble.

We began the year with one french fry. We ended it with me watching him go into the school building with his books. I pop his storytelling tape into the truck's tape player and listen to the music and the drums. I'm sitting in another school parking lot. I am not searching anyone's car for guns. I am, however, returning a wounded one back into the wild.

# 14

# Oñate's Foot

*T*HERE'S A NEW STORY being told among the Indians. I
cannot testify that the story is wholly accurate, only that it's being told, embellished with flourishes perhaps as the story is explained to children. House to house. Family to family. Cooking
fire to cooking fire. Bar to bar. Powwow to powwow. It's the
kind of story that will make it from the small context of a joke
all the way to the larger structures of mythology. It isn't a story
that is being written down or told to white children who will lis-

ten. It's the kind of story you would have a difficult time getting Indians to share with anyone outside the confines of the group. It's an Indian story and as such it's about two not unrelated things: symbolism and survival. It's not a story Indians think white people will ever understand, but it's out there now making its anthropological way to the truth found in other stories— the ones that explain the past and make sense of the unexplainable.

It is the story of the conquistador and how he lost his foot.

It is a modern story tossed about all the conventions of every other Indian story that is as ancient as the hills. It is a story tossed about the waves, tossed about malcontented confrontations, a story of soldiers and armor glinting silver in the sun, tossed about a desert of wishes, tossed and tangled with the branches and roots of other ancient stories, grinding its slow way through chaos, through a battle with blood and the screaming of horses, through hot places where nothing stirs, through the opposing needs of individuals where defeat is not so much a game you play but a path you hike through wreckage, and survival is a reenactment that your mother tells of beautiful things gone mad, and rapids, twisting, stirring, swimming in the constellations of myths like some great pain is forever freed and dances now along roads of austere nerves where hunger sinks its teeth into the belly. It is a story imbued and exemplified with the daring actions of its heroes.

In this Indian tale Roy Laughter is a radical Indian although he denies it. Roy is a criminal, too.

It is not an accident that the concept of the criminal and the concept of the radical Indian would find their way to Indian mythology via a modern story's circuitous route.

. . .

Roy committed a crime that was the talk of New Mexico for at least a month. He helped cut the foot off the statue of the conquistador.

Roy tells me that crime is everywhere.

When Roy hits the city he makes sure to carry plastic bags so when his dog poops in a public park he can immediately clean up after her. If you don't clean up after your animal you can receive a ticket. The fine can be as much as three hundred dollars. That's one expensive poop.

This is the Indian part of the story, and a contradiction, too, designed to get a laugh from the obedient children who hear it. The notion of an Indian male who cleans up after his dog poops in a public park is often perceived as hilarious.

Like most criminals, Roy doesn't think of himself as a criminal. He has never been in trouble with the law. He has never been to prison. He has received speeding tickets. That's about it.

Roy's last speeding ticket was in 1979. He was coming down Ski Valley Road from Taos Ski Valley. It's real easy to speed here because you're descending at a rapid rate. People have died on this road. Roy was going fifty in a zone marked for thirty-five. He hasn't received another speeding ticket in twenty years. Roy avoids trouble with the law, and trouble in general, whenever he can. Trouble is usually not worth the grief it causes.

Roy Laughter committed a crime in northern New Mexico.

Some say it was a crime of passion.

The Oñate Center in Alcalde, New Mexico, is just north of Espanola and south of Taos. Roy's part of northern New Mexico is perhaps one of the most beautiful places in the world. The Sangre de Cristo Mountains here were so named by the conquering, bloodthirsty Spaniards because the sunsets reminded the invading Europeans of the blood of Christ. While the mountains that surround the Taos Valley are stunning, the poverty that pervades here is just as stunning. Where there's poverty, there's ignorance. Most people who live here cannot even tell you who Don Juan de Oñate was.

The Oñate Center seems small, somewhat poor, somewhat spiritless, and seems to struggle in its attempt to make its historical and ethnic point. Espanola is a place of fast-food joints and used-tire joints with a Wal-Mart on one side of town. There are more than a few drive-up liquor stores. Buy your bottle and never have to leave the car. Rap music booms at you as you drive through town. What town there is. Espanola is not a tourist destination. The place feels a little worn around the edges. It is not a place you would expect to find a cultural center dedicated to anything, let alone a point of view, because the culture that surrounds this place seems exhausted, almost broken by the poverty it bears. The Oñate Center is dedicated to the memory and the achievements of Don Juan de Oñate, who began colonizing the region for Spain in 1595.

Oñate was a Spanish aristocrat and one of the richest men in the world at the time the Southwest was conquered.

Arriving at El Paso del Norte, Oñate ceremoniously took possession of all the country north of Juarez: "In the name of the Most Holy Trinity, and the Undivided Eternal Unity, Deity and Majesty, Father, Son, and Holy Ghost . . . and of his most sacred and blessed mother, the Holy Virgin Mary . . . Mother of God, Sun, Moon, North Star, guide, and advocate of humanity; and in honor of the Seraphic Father, San Francisco . . . patriarch of the poor, whom I adopt as my patrons, advocates, guides, defenders, and intercessors . . . I, Don Juan de Oñate, Governor and Captain General and Adelantado of New Mexico, and of its kingdoms and provinces, as well as those in their vicinity and contiguous thereto, as settler, discoverer, and pacifier of them and of the said kingdoms, by order of the King our Lord . . .

*"I take this land."*

Don Juan de Oñate came marching with his army of soldiers, with its banners and its harquebuses, with priests, poets, and *carretas.* Then, as now, houses piled up out of the earth, their rafters cut from the cottonwoods that grew thick on the floodplain. Up and down the Rio Jemez there were towns, and also along the Galisteo. On the rich alluvial plain of Rio Abaja, Indian field touched Indian field. Six-colored corn, ears of it as long as a man's forearm, beans, squashes, melons, cotton. Cicuyé, a walled city boasting five hundred fighting men, was a focus of population along the Pecos. The valley of Espanola was filled with villages. Abiquiu was a pueblo, also Ranchos de Taos. Taos was the chief pueblo of the Tiguas. Oñate brought the cross—not the cross of forgiveness, but the cross that was the terror of the Roman slaves.

His wealth was based in silver mining and slavery. There is a large bronze sculpture of Don Juan de Oñate on his horse that sits outside the cultural center. The sculpture, very much in the tradition of grand, romanticized European art, portrays Oñate astride his running steed, holding a weapon in his hand, dressed in his Spanish cape and his conquistador's armor. There is a terror to the thing. The figure of Don Juan de Oñate seems heroic and eulogizes the conquistador as a man of action. The figure on the horse is handsome and vigorous, whereas the real Oñate is depicted in Spanish paintings of the time as somewhat delicate and sallow. A clipped beard accentuates the impression of fragility. But the figure on the horse projects the image of a strong, agile, and athletic man. It is a sculptural rendering of a machismo that never was. The romantic image of the straining horse almost overwhelms the image of the man riding the horse, yet it is the boots and the exaggerated size of the spurs the conquistador is wearing that imply a particular authority as to who and what Don Juan de Oñate was.

Don Juan de Oñate was a butcher.

Don Juan de Oñate was a sadist.

Roy Laughter would cut his leg off at the ankle.

The year 1998 was the four hundredth anniversary of Oñate's arrival in New Mexico. Like crime, celebrations were everywhere.

"We are the sons of our past, but we are also the fathers of our future," Spain's first vice president, Francisco Alvarez-Cascos, claims. "Those in charge of government cannot revise history."

History is a cause for celebration. The Spanish had been here before. Vásquez de Coronado had explored and conquered the territory for the king of Spain as early as 1540. Warfare conducted against the native peoples of the region was particularly brutal. Both Coronado and Oñate sought gold, slaves, and the Indians' conversion to Catholicism. History in this mostly forgotten part of America begins with the arrival of the Spanish.

Nothing that happened before the arrival of the Europeans matters.

New Mexico is one of those places, a blend of cultures unto itself, that defies the definitions of its origins. Behind the Navajo hogan of Roy Laughter there are big red rocks that depict the images of bighorn sheep.

There is a big rock called El Morro on the Navajo Nation. There is a sweetwater spring near the base of the rock, and it's known that many travelers over the centuries stopped here to drink. The name of Don Juan de Oñate is clearly etched into the rock. What's interesting about this graffiti is that it's not too far from other, older images etched into the same rock. Images of Kokopelli with his penis and his flute. In some of these humorous drawings, Kokopelli's penis *is* his flute. Other ancient images feature hands, wild beasts, and creatures that have disappeared from the face of history and the earth. At the top of El Morro rock there is an abandoned Indian village. No one lives there now. It is a spectacular place to watch the sun set. You can almost hear the voices of the People in the vast, haunting aloneness of the place.

No one knows what happened to the People of El Morro.

Who from invisibility had come to play his flute alone? History is mute. We only have pit houses and kivas.

Perhaps they had no history. Perhaps they never existed. Perhaps history began with the arrival of Don Juan de Oñate.

History is now. You are your history.

Roy Laughter and his brother prepare for a tourist trip to the Oñate Center in Alcalde. There will be four people in all riding in the cab of Roy's pickup. The Indians wish to educate themselves. It will be crowded, but they are used to it.

Jimmy Dog, a friend, arrives at Ray's hogan early in the morning. It is still dark. The Navajo stars are as clear and blue as diamonds. Jimmy Dog has never been to Alcalde. He has never seen the statue of Oñate.

The three Indian men drive from Hosta Butte to the interstate that takes them east to Acoma. Roy's dog squeezes in here, too.

It's already a little crowded. They have yet to add one more.

It is a four-butt pickup truck.

Plus the dog.

Acoma is one of the oldest continuously inhabited cities in North America. It was here generations and generations before the Spanish arrived. By the time the Spanish discovered it, Acoma was old. Like the vanished village at the top of El Morro, it sits at the summit of an enormous rock. Going to Acoma is going back in time. The barking of dogs. Roy's dog immediately feels at home. The smell of bread in adobe ovens. The warm feel of the sun against the earth colors of the Indian village. Their friend Ray Redshoes lives here. It is still too early for most folks to be up and running, but there's a subliminal buzz to the village as people go about their morning chores.

People here still blow corn dust into the morning wind as a way of communicating thanks for the life to be lived that day.

Ray Redshoes feeds Roy Laughter, Roy's brother, and Jimmy Dog breakfast. "Would you like to see where Oñate cut off the feet of the Indians?" Ray asks. The brothers say yes.

Ray Redshoes shows Jimmy Dog and the Laughter brothers around Acoma. He points out the various places where his Acoma ancestors once defended their village and their people against the men who had arrived from Europe to enslave them. It is not a history taught in white public schools. It never happened. The Acoma remember. The stories of how their ancestors stood and fought the coming onslaught have been incorporated into the contemporary mythology of what is still an oral culture. Ray Redshoes shows the small group where the young Acoma boys were run through with Spanish swords. This is now a sacred spot. Ray Redshoes points out the spot where the Elders were beheaded. He shows the assembled Indian men where Don Juan de Oñate had the right feet of male Indians amputated after the Spanish had defeated the Acoma Pueblo in 1599.

Cutting off the feet of the Acoma Indians is only one of the cruelties that were perpetrated against them. The women were raped. Pregnant women were disemboweled. Young men were publicly castrated. Old people and children were put in cages and fed to vicious dogs. Babies had their brains bashed in with rocks. Medicine men were burned at the stake. The "discoverers" of New Mexico conducted a systematic campaign of terror against the people and the cultures they "discovered."

It was not a good time for native peoples. Then, as now.

Four hundred years later, methods of warfare have changed, but war itself is still very much the same story.

Today the war against the Indians continues as a cultural experiment to be celebrated.

It is a history that is ignored. It is a history never published. It is a story that cannot be told. White people will not allow it. It is the history of the Indians.

Ray Redshoes brings sandwiches and a hacksaw.

Their goal is to cut off the right foot of the bronze statue of Don Juan de Oñate.

This might be more trouble than a speeding ticket on Ski Valley Road.

Roy Laughter can feel his heart beating almost wildly in his chest as he drives to Albuquerque, then north toward Santa Fe. Each Indian man understands that he is about to engage in a criminal act of extraordinary vandalism. What they will do is a symbolic act they want to echo throughout New Mexico. The four are mostly silent. Ray Redshoes pops a tape into the truck's tape player. The music of the Acoma.

There is something about the music of the Acoma that is almost sad.

The Indian men eat their sandwiches in the plaza in Santa

Fe across the street from the Palace of the Governors, where the Spanish ruled New Mexico with an iron fist.

"I'm glad I had this idea," Roy Laughter's brother remarks.

They all look at him incredulously.

Jimmy Dog thought he himself had suggested it.

It was Ray Redshoes's hacksaw.

Roy Laughter would be the getaway driver.

He is now a criminal. He has conspired.

Indians from everywhere sit on the sidewalk and sell their jewelry. There is much talk among them. Many are animated. A few seem quiet, resigned, and depressed.

The four conspirators are in no hurry. What they have to do must take place in darkness.

They drive through Espanola, landscape of the lowrider. (*Hermano, camarada: persona que se identifica con un grupo, esp. racial o de clase económica baja.*) The people here are very poor. We are the brown people and they are the brown people, they are the brown people and we are the half-red people, too, and we all live side by side in a culture dominated by the whites. It remains an uneasy alliance. Somehow Indians and white people must begin the process of seeing history for what it really was instead of seeing visions of a heroic machismo that was as much a lie then as it is now. If we are ever to change anything about the reality we live in, we have to start seeing where that reality came from, how it evolved, and we have to stop seeing it within the glorious confines of an illusion that never was.

Our romanticized machismo is still killing the likes of us.

Our romanticized machismo is our inability to connect to the women we love.

Our romanticized machismo is our inability to connect to the men we love.

Our romanticized machismo is our inability to connect to the children we father.

Our romanticized machismo is our alcoholism and our addictions and our tattoos and our prison cells and our concrete prison yards and the violence of the gang.

Our romanticized machismo must be redefined.

It doesn't work. The center cannot hold. True machismo is never rape.

We need new stories to get tossed about the waves.

Roy Laughter drives past the Oñate Center in Alcalde. The Indian men in the truck see the statue they plan to deface. It's going to be a piece of cake. Even in the light of day there are hardly any people around. This time there will be no one to defend the macho integrity of Don Juan de Oñate.

They have dinner at the El Pueblo in El Prado. They can smell the piñon burning in the air.

They do not drive down Ski Valley Road. Too many State Police.

They drive back to Alcalde. It is dark now. They are alone.

There are no other vehicles in the parking lot.

"I want to do this," Ray Redshoes says. Ray Redshoes is an Acoma.

The bronze statue, so solid looking in its charging fierceness, is hollow. Roy Laughter doesn't know why he didn't think of the thing as being hollow. Somehow without thinking about it he assumed the thing was solid. He knows nothing about sculpting statues. He feels nothing for the artist who created this. He does not know why. Perhaps because the art glorifies something so devastating. Perhaps because it serves to make something like the Holocaust okay. Ray Redshoes's hacksaw makes short work

of it. Don Juan de Oñate now looks appropriately crippled.
The Indian men do not celebrate what they do. They don't feel
good about it. They know this: it's way past time for something
to be said. The romanticizing of such men as the conquistadors
must end here.

The foot with its boot and its spur is heavy. They lug it back
to the truck.

The drive back to Acoma is a long one. The bronze foot of Don
Juan de Oñate rolls around the back of Roy Laughter's pickup
as he negotiates the curves up and down the mountains to the
old pueblo.

He is a criminal now.

They say crime is everywhere.

I do not have the guts to write any of this until some time after the crime was committed. Okay, a *long* time after the crime
was committed. I am hoping the statute of limitations might
take effect.

Their arrival with the conquistador's foot was anticipated by
many people. There was a hush to the group of Acoma who
came to meet them.

Children are allowed to touch the foot of the conqueror.

The men must hide the foot. What they have done will set off
a firestorm of controversy.

At some point they will wish the controversy would go away.

The authorities are looking for whoever did this.

"I told you they would," my dog informs me.

The Associated Press proclaims that a delegation from Spain
seeks to settle a four-hundred-year-old grudge with New Mexico's Indian tribes over brutality by explorers who began con-

quering the region in the 1500s. The cutting off of the statue's foot is denounced everywhere in the media. The executive director of the state's Office of Indian Affairs claims something must be done.

Roy Laughter sort of likes being denounced as a vandal.

*Vandal* is better than *writer*.

That edge he seeks.

"Something has been done," Ray Redshoes says. "We have buried Oñate's foot. Only we know where."

If the truth be known, Roy Laughter has forgotten exactly where. He couldn't find it in the dark if he had to.

The state of New Mexico organizes 185 events to celebrate the conquest by the Spanish. The delegation from Spain that wants to meet with Indian tribes in the area includes Spain's First Vice President Francisco Alvarez-Cascos. The Spanish government has requested a face-to-face meeting. Many tribal leaders see no point in meeting with the Spanish. But I know Indians. I am one, halved. The Indians will meet with the Spanish because they're curious. Nothing more. Nothing less. Not too unlike the old days. The Roman Catholic Church also wants to reconcile with the Indians and will hold a special mass. The Roman Catholic Church still seeks converts among the Indians. "We should remember the good things," says Archbishop Michael Sheehan of Santa Fe.

"What good things?" Ray Redshoes wonders. "My great-grandfather was a slave."

So far, no Indian leader has agreed to attend such a meeting with the Spanish.

But they will. The Indians are too polite. Who from invisibility has come to play his flute alone?

Alvarez-Cascos plans to present a cane of office from King Juan Carlos to the governor of San Juan Pueblo in commemoration of Spanish royal forces and the Indians they murdered four hundred years ago. While centuries have passed, resentment continues to smolder. The tribal sovereignty Native Americans fought so hard for remains a turbulent social issue even today.

Your history is now. You are your history.

The Holocaust did not take place in an encyclopedia.

Writing this — confessing to knowledge of a crime — scares the hell out of me. I am not courageous. Who knows — I may not include this essay in the book I am writing it for. Like many of the other essays, I might set it aside. Better safe than sorry. I am a coward.

My dog just shakes her head. "It's only a story," she says.

"We are reminded," Regis Pecos, the state's executive director of the Office of Indian Affairs, says, "that our fight will be as vicious as those people who have gone on before us. Like them, we are not willing to compromise a way of life."

Officialdom has spoken, yet officialdom speaks with many tongues.


Jimmy Dog and the Laughter brothers sit around the fire of Ray Redshoes while Ray Redshoes tells the assembled children many stories of the Acoma. Being at Acoma is like going back in time. History is a living organism. Everyone here has had a chance to touch and wonder at the metal hardness of Oñate's foot.

The history of the Indians is the blood that flows like a river to the ocean.

The Acoma eyes of Ray Redshoes seem very far away.

You with those eyes of earth colors telling me to come home, against my breast the rigor of a thousand suns.

Ray Redshoes speaks: "On the mesa that cold night there

was much dancing and the reveling of our people until dawn. The drums and chanting could be clearly heard by the Spanish soldiers who could only have had snatches of sleep in the bitter freezing of the weather. They must have wondered what the morning would bring. Our chief's name was Kho-Ka-Cha-Ni and he watched all of this silently. The entire Spanish camp was up before dawn as if they were happy now to get a difficult job done. The day was clear and raw and high-desert winter. As a few Spanish soldiers were finishing their breakfast, some of their horses wandered to frozen water at the base of the rock. Our warriors who were on that side of the mesa attacked. The conquistadors opened fire. Our warriors fell. Others scattered. That night the world was saturated with the screaming of our people. The beheading of our children. The beheading of the Elders. The raping of our women. Don Juan de Oñate ordered as many Acoma as possible to be hanged. The wars against us would continue for a very long time. This is how the battle of Acoma begins."

It is not, however, where history ends. Navajo, my Australian cattle dog, and I drive to Denver to witness the governor of Colorado sign into law a bill requiring that Indian culture be taught in history classes. I cover this event as a reporter, hoping to sell my article to papers all over the Southwest. It took the efforts of many Indian activists to get this bill through the Colorado legislature.

"It's finally here," Judy Knight-Frank says. Knight-Frank is the chairwoman of the Ute Mountain Ute Tribe.

The governor calls the bill good law. "It's important that the unique contributions of Native Americans are recognized. It's important to present history accurately," he says.

It's all very civilized.

How will knowing about the real history of the conquistadors, and what they did to the Indians of the Southwest, help
some poor Ute high school student who lives in a tarpaper
shack outside Cortez? How will having an understanding of his
place in the scheme of things allow him to pull himself up by his
bootstraps?

I don't know. Sometimes you have to push for what feels
right.

Sometimes you discover things in the encyclopedia.

Sometimes you have to demand that the tools for learning *be
there*.

Symbolism is everything.

No matter what, there is always a price to the ticket.

Navajo and I leave Denver and drive back to the Navajo Nation by way of Alcalde, New Mexico. The right foot of Don
Juan de Oñate is still missing.

Like a wound.

It is a story tossed about the waves, tossed about malcontented confrontations, a story of soldiers and armor glinting silver in the sun, tossed about a desert of wishes, tossed and tangled with the branches and roots of other ancient stories,
grinding its slow way through chaos, through a battle with
blood and the screaming of horses, through hot places where
nothing stirs, through the opposing needs of individuals where
defeat is not so much a game you play but a path you hike
through wreckage, and survival is a reenactment that your
mother tells of beautiful things gone mad, and rapids, twisting,
stirring, swimming in the constellations of myths like some
great pain is forever freed and dances now along roads of austere nerves where hunger sinks its teeth into the belly.

It is a story being told house to house. Child to child. Cooking fire to cooking fire. Making its circuitous way from story into myth.

I wonder if criminal mischief is a misdemeanor. They say criminals are always attracted back to the scene of the crime. I drive away. Repelled.

# 15

# A Movie Lives Inside My Head

*T*HERE'S A MOVIE that lives inside my head. Image: Tommy Nothing Fancy and I are standing at the side of a lonesome desert road with mountains in the distance. This is a place of rusted wire fences and jackrabbits. There is some green here. But not a lot. It's that middle place between the desert and the dust the desert creates when it decides it is big enough to feed itself. It creates more desert. Tommy is a young man now. We are waiting for the bus that will arrive to take Tommy Nothing

Fancy away to college. We are wearing jeans and cowboy boots. Tommy has one of his nice shirts on. There is a conservatism and a shyness that still runs through his Navajo bones like a lightning flash that scrapes across the face of the desert. My movie comes in brilliant Technicolor and the magical ability to remember what might have been.

He has one bag of stuff.

We are unsure of what to say, so mainly we say nothing. His arrogance lingers a bit in the boy who is now a man. In the movie Tommy is taking off for Boston. It's a Boston college. In the movie inside my head he is determined to get as good an education as can be had. There is no such thing as fetal alcohol syndrome. In the movie all the bad things ultimately get contained as opposed to what goes on in real life. In real life we never made it all the way to Boston. I was the one who aspired for him. I wanted him to have what he wanted. In this respect I am no different from any other man who happens to be someone's dad. In the movie, Tommy's going off to college.

He's still something of the cowboy, though. You can see it in him. At seventeen he's still a little gawky and not above saying things like, "Gee, Dad."

My presence here at the side of this road causes him to be somewhat uncomfortable. He wants to be independent now. He thinks I should go home.

I'm not ready to let him go just yet.

I do not know when I will see him again.

In the movie he gave up fishing. He just grew out of it and I had to learn how to fish alone. In the movie a dialogue goes on between the two of us that is unbroken by traffic or wildlife. We are the wildlife.

"I can get on the bus by myself, you know. Why don't you

leave me here and I'll get on the bus as soon as it comes along. It probably hasn't left Wal-Mart yet."

"No, I'm going to stay." I give him my best and most somber Old Stoneface look. He sighs in exasperation.

I have to let him go.

But I do not know how. I feel as if I came all the way out here in the desert without my tools. Something I would never do willingly.

My tools go where I go. I am nothing without them.

Out here in the desert, memory plays tricks like Coyote the trickster who howls his objections and mine to a yellowish peyote moon. Out here where the road shimmers like water sizzles in emptiness and paths you take are not always the path you wanted to take but there it was. It was a path that somehow presented itself to you and you did your damnedest not to get lost on it. I have to leave soon. I must return to the reservation like I have always returned to the reservation as if reservations might be islands in the stream which is what reservations really are. Tommy Nothing Fancy survived the reservation. Now off to college and all the paths that will in turn present themselves resplendently like jewels made from silver and turquoise and the tongues of gods.

Still no bus.

"It wasn't like this," he says. "In real life it was very, very different."

"I know that," I say. "Tell me, what becomes of us in real life?"

He grins. "In real life you moved to Florida because you couldn't take the Navajo winter anymore. You know, your arthritis."

I laughed. "Do I still fish?" I asked.

"Yes," he said. "Some things never change."

"But you gave it up. Or maybe it was me you gave up on."

"I never give up. You know that."

But I noted that he had not packed a rod or a reel anywhere in his stuff. One bag.

"I know that," I said.

"*Girls.*" We both said it. There would have been *girls*. The place would have been full of them.

We both laughed.

In the movie he looks away off in the distance for the bus. In the movie there are logical conclusions to things. Car chases. There are things that never happened. Like girls. And Boston. Everything gets concluded in its rightful place. The bad guy gets what's coming to him, and the good guy gets, yes, the girl. Tommy Nothing Fancy was a good guy no matter which way you looked at it or him. This bus simply isn't going to arrive until I leave. Obviously, he knows that.

He grows impatient with me again.

He will get over it.

In the movie we hug and wonder what will become of us. In this respect, real life and the movies are similar. I get back into Old Big Wanda.

My dog, Navajo, rests her head on my lap. I cannot see. But I force myself to look in the rearview mirror. He was standing there. A Navajo Indian. I could never ask more from him than that.

# 16

# Navajo Rose
# and the Codetalker

*T*HERE ARE some things I do not care to know about. How to butcher a sheep is one of those things.

Navajo Rose and her grandfather lived down on the reservation dirt road not far from where I was living on the Checkerboard in New Mexico. Navajo Rose is one tough woman. She has to be.

When it rains the road she lives on turns into a sea of mud. Big Mud. There is no escape.

Navajo Rose has to put chains on the tires of her pickup. You put the chains on—no small task, that—and then you drive very slowly to your hogan. Navajo Rose owns a wolf hybrid. No small task, that, too. She has to keep one eye on the animal all the time. In an area where almost everyone owns sheep, wolf hybrids would eat all of them. Navajo Rose has trained the dog so he responds to her when she speaks to him in Navajo. The animal can come, stay, sit, and heel, and unlike the other, freer reservation dogs, knows what a leash is all about. I had never seen a dog trained to Navajo commands. That dog knows more Athabaskan than I do. The story of Navajo Rose and how she got the dog is a simple one: he just showed up. "Almost starved to death," Rose explains.

So she kept him. Owning a wolf hybrid is a challenge but Rose seems up to it. That dog adores Navajo Rose.

Rose never puts the animal in the back of the pickup the way other reservation dogs ride around. The wolf hybrid sits in the cab of Navajo Rose's vehicle like he's something of a king. There is indeed a royal attitude to this dog. She named him King, too.

"Don't pet King," she tells people who are curious. I take her admonition seriously, and I do not pet King. Wolf hybrids do not necessarily make good pets—the mix of the wild and the civilized remains an uneasy alliance—and Navajo Rose has to supervise the animal at all times. She does not seem to mind in any way, and King follows her around the hogan and into White People Town whenever Rose makes the trip. The Big Mud can be something of an inconvenience. Navajo Rose wishes she lived on a road that was paved. "Maybe someday the tribe will pave this one," she says, and she laughs when she says it.

It will never happen, and Navajo Rose keeps her tire chains in the back of the pickup.

Rose cares for the man who is her grandfather, who was a codetalker during the Second World War. He served in the South Pacific during a time when the Navajo soldier was used in radio communications—transmitting messages in Navajo—and the Japanese never did figure out the language or break the code. It is a generation of men who are disappearing.

I call him Codetalker because his ancient eyes now tell stories, too. The stories at first seem simple, but they are never as simple as they seem.

There is a sophistication to the stories that at first appears to be what white people call primitive, as they rate cultures in hierarchies like totems on a totem pole. But what is misunderstood as primitive is instead sophisticated like the totem pole.

On the outside, Navajo Rose looks like any other ordinary Navajo woman, with her grandfather on her arm, her animal beside her, walking paths that were laid out and traversed by native people preceding the Anasazi. Inside the living, bloody history, a story takes its strength from something unexplainable and hidden deep within. There is nothing ordinary about a Navajo woman and the enigma she is to the universe.

Codetalker and Rose take frequent walks on the Navajo path between where I live and where Rose has lived all her life. Sometimes they walk the wolf hybrid, who seems to relish the outdoor walks. The dog is not allowed to roam loose. It's not kept on a chain, but it goes where Rose and Codetalker go. "This path, you know," Rose explains, "has existed for centuries."

My eyes scoff at the notion of centuries.

"No, it's really old," Rose insists. "Today the roads go where there used to be paths. The paved road into town used to be a path."

Codetalker does not venture out on the paths by himself much but seems content to walk with Rose.

Rose brought me Navajo tacos made with mutton. She had even butchered the sheep. A tree in back of Rose's hogan is filled with sheepskins exposed to the weather. It's odd to see this tree with the skins hanging from it, but it's not odd to Rose. Every so often Rose will sell all the sheepskins, and she gets good money for them. Her hogan has many sheepskins around the floor like rugs, and she has several Navajo rugs hanging from the wall. One was made by Codetalker's grandmother and it is very old. Rose is a traditional Navajo cook, but she is not a traditional Navajo.

Rose is a Christian.

She has been saved.

Every summer there's a tent revival on her land. I don't know where the preachers come from. But most of them are white.

A traditional Navajo believes in Changing Woman. A Christian Navajo believes in Changing Woman and Jesus, too. Rose covers all her bases.

Rose wants to make me Navajo tacos because I am squeamish about butchering sheep. She laughs and says I think of sheep as pets. The Navajo do not see their livestock as pets. Rose said she would come over with hot Navajo tacos if I would teach her how to read and write in English. Quid pro quo.

"I want to be able to read the Bible," she says.

How someone can graduate from high school and not be able to read is beyond me, but there it is. Rose went all the way to the twelfth grade. Nevertheless she cannot read and she cannot write in English. Her hot Navajo tacos are very good. So is her fry bread. She tempts me with food, but what I don't tell her is that I would teach her how to read and write in English for free.

I wonder how she got a driver's license, but I say nothing.

It would not surprise me to know that Rose does not have a driver's license. She does, however, have a radar scanner in her truck which beeps when law enforcement is clocking her. "That's when I slow down," she says.

This is a remote area of the reservation, and not being able to drive would be something of a hardship.

Teaching Rose to read and write in English is not difficult. She is very bright and learns fast. "They didn't think much of me in high school," she says. "We were shipped away to an Indian school in Oregon."

When Rose talks about being shipped away the lines around her mouth grow tight. Navajo Rose didn't think much of being shipped away.

The next time she went into White People Town I went along because I wanted Rose to see the library. She had never been inside a library before. She is impressed with all the books. There are computers, too. Rose is a little intimidated by the computers. We ignore them. Rose looks at books about religion. She gets a library card with her name on it. She is amazed you can check out books for free.

I find a book about the Navajo codetalkers who helped America win the war with the Japanese.

The book has pictures of some of the old men.

I want Rose to know that there's more to read than the Bible. The library has several versions of the Bible. Rose is quite intrigued.

Rose sold some sheepskins and got a Primestar satellite dish this year. "Codetalker," she explained, "he likes them shows."

Rose grows amazing Indian corn. When she talks about the corn her eyes light up. Rose could fill the back of her pickup with all the corn she grows. She brought me some Indian corn ears.

You don't see Navajo Rose out and about so much anymore now that she's a card-carrying member of the library and has a satellite dish. Navajo Rose is a modern Indian. Now she reads and watches them shows with Codetalker, who does not read but pets the wolf hybrid who lives with them. When the snow melts and Big Mud comes Rose puts her chains on her truck tires and drives up the dirt road (now a sea of liquid earth) to my house and delivers hot Navajo tacos.

Quid pro quo.

Sometimes she brings lists of words she does not understand. I bought Rose a dictionary, but still she brings her lists. Her fry bread melts in your mouth like butter on a summer afternoon.

To prove to me that the Navajo paths were as ancient as she said they were, Rose took me to a point along the path that connects us where pieces of old pottery litter the ground. The pottery is not Navajo but is more likely to be from Pueblo Indians, now gone. The pieces of pottery (which we leave right where we found them) all have fanciful inklike patterns and designs painted on them. "Makes you wonder what we'll leave behind," Rose said.

I know this: among the ephemeral things we will leave behind us will be the stories we tell. Like pottery shards left scattered in the dirt.

You are your history, too.

Navajo Rose does not see herself at any future time being connected to a male. We have discussed the notion of husbands some. Rose is not an optimist. She claims that husbands are a heap of trouble. "More trouble than a wolf."

The mix of the wild and the civilized makes an uneasy alliance. One learns to balance both things, and one does not necessarily have to be a wolf hybrid to do it well. Rose has offered to show me how to butcher a sheep. She thinks my squeamishness is silly. I get the general idea, and know that it is done with knives, but there are some things I remain unwilling to really understand.

# 17

# Go Fish

*H*IS WAS the deep silence that does not endeavor to explain itself in words. His was the deep silence of the lake, where the light slants down from a sun of lambent red. His were the singing secrets of the lake where fat crabs come ashore to feed at night like clusters of blackbirds that move swiftly in the darkness back into the canyons of the lake. His were the eyes of some unmerciful god imprisoned in his split, uninhabitable head where the edges of his dreams speak in torrents of tongues. He hovers like a shadow floating on water.

His eyes were the silence of the caves hidden high in the mountains all around us.

His was the cold of the snow-fed lake and the burning heat of the summer afternoon.

My cousin was deaf and he didn't speak much although sometimes he made strange sorts of strangulated sounds. You could sometimes hear his voice when he laughed. You could hear weird, anguished sounds when he cried, too. My cousin lived away at school. I did not know where the school was. I never asked. It didn't matter. Sometimes he would be with us in the summer when all us kids congregated like a raggedy knot. My cousin could speak with his hands and his fingers. In school he spoke in American Sign Language. But we didn't know American Sign Language, so when he was with us he spoke in Indian sign. Indian sign is conceptual. He was a couple of years younger than I was.

His fingers were the horses that ran away over the hills into the trees.

I don't know who first taught me some Indian sign. I think it was my grandfather, who was a commanding presence in our lives. The lives of us kids. Our grandfather knew all the signs. You use your fingers and your hands and the essence of simplicity.

My cousin used his eyes, too, in ways that surrounded you with no escape.

The Indian sign for fish is made by first making the sign for water. You cup your left hand as if you are drinking water. Then you hold your right hand flat near the waist and you move your hand sinuously as if it's a swimming fish. You don't have to be a rocket scientist to get Indian sign. It is a language of great antiquity.

Indian sign was created so tribes who spoke different languages could communicate. Today it is mainly another lost language, one of many, and not many people can sign in Indian sign.

My cousin and I used Indian sign to communicate when we went fishing, which was just about every day.

Hearing sounds and speaking in words are not necessities when you fish.

It was a mistake to assume that my cousin's universe was a tenuous universe of silence or emptiness. In fact it was a fluid universe of movement, affinity, alliances, sublime extravagances, evanescent pleasures, rendezvous with first-blush auroras, mornings, voyages, mercurial vagrancies, and a momentum forged in rampant elevation, up, up, standing on my shoulders in the water, vaulting circumfusion bubbled forth, embodied in a gulp of waves. His feet slipping from my shoulders and we both fell. It was a mistake to assume his silence was a heaviness, when in fact his silence was a gravity balanced light against the ballast of the world.

Two boys out on a small rowboat early in the morning on a lake. Fishing for food. Wisps of fog clinging to the surface of the water like the suggestion of a kiss. It was a heavy responsibility fishing for food. It was up to us to feed the family, and there were at least a dozen other kids and various adults who would be hoongry, too. There was only one boat and we were in it. Up at dawn when the morning monsters stretch and yawn and the surface of the lake is only broken by the occasional rebellious jumping of a fish. To break the surface of the lake was to reason with the sanity of the thing. Although my cousin couldn't hear the splash, he never missed the jumping of a fish. What he couldn't hear, he saw. He always knew a fish had jumped before I did. We would row over to where the fish were jumping. You wanted to catch a rebellious fish. Lazy fish weren't worth the effort it took to catch them, but a rebellious fish would jump right into a net.

The fishing really began the night before and sometimes the day before if we were using grasshoppers for bait. The night before we went fishing we'd go hunting for night crawlers. Big worms almost the size of snakes. Out with our flashlights in the ditches by the road where the night crawlers emerged from their hiding places in the earth. That this moving flesh, the worm, could live underneath the ground was a thing of wonder, and we told the little kids that we ate worms. We often bragged we could do things we could not do. The little kids did not quite believe us but they weren't really sure. In a world where anything was possible it was conceivable we ate worms raw. When one of the little kids ate a worm so he could be like us, we got into trouble. There was an antidote for the trouble we could get into, and that antidote was to send us fishing.

Go fish, boy.

You have to catch a lot of fish to feed almost twenty people.

There was fish for breakfast. There was fish for lunch. There was fish for supper, too.

It not only kept us busy but kept us intimately connected to the group. What we did kept the group fed. We fished every day. And we liked it. We took our responsibilities seriously — we were positioned with the men, although we were of the women — and we caught as many fish as we could. The fruits of our labor were not mysterious. We could see how well we had done at every meal. We belonged. We had a place. Putting food on the table was up to us.

The boat is old and speckled with the many colors it has been painted over the broad span of years. The oars dip down into the cool deepness of the water and then you have to pull. You find yourself unconsciously doing this as to make no sound. Sounds from the rusty oar locks seemed to echo from some unseen place across the lake. My cousin was the perfect fishing buddy because he was always so quiet. His eyes said most of the things he had to say. There were volumes in his vision. If he caught your eye he kept you there in the quiet resolution of his gaze. In this respect he was like the lake itself. A living thing. Not a thing of deafness but a thing of sensuous reciprocity.

We sincerely believed (because our grandfather had told us this) that in order to catch fish you couldn't scare them with unnecessary noise. My cousin sits in the stern of the boat as I row the two of us across the lake to a spot where we think many morning fish have jumped. My cousin's hands are caked with dirt and his fingernails are cracked. The dirt is from the night before when we dug through the cool earth with our hands for the worms that would be our bait. I have a coffee can filled with popping grasshoppers. My cousin makes a sign as if he's holding a mirror to his face. He is telling me that the lake is like a mirror. We have cane poles and bobbers. Fishing at its most basic level, restrained and inornate.

My cousin's clothes are barely rags.

No shoes. Afternoon legs to dangle in the water. This does not help you catch fish but it does serve to keep you cool. We jump in the water when we have to pee. Back in the boat which doesn't quite capsize. I am catching fish. One after the other. Sunfish, perch, and bluegill. In Florida they call them bream. I am using grasshoppers and a sinker. My cousin sticks to worms and catches nothing.

I gloat just a little.

By late afternoon my cousin's anguish grows. I have caught all the fish and he has caught nothing. Not even a nibble. The boy is very stubborn. He doesn't like grasshoppers because he doesn't like the way they leak brown tobacco juice when you stick them with a hook. But the worms just aren't working. It's a grasshopper kind of day. It took me all of yesterday afternoon to catch these insects, and the fish love them, and the fish are biting. But not worms. I make the Indian sign for mule. You extend your hands alongside your ears, fingers pointed upward. My cousin is stubborn like a mule. To make the Indian sign for disgust, you make the signs for heart and tired. The head is then turned to one side and the idea is conveyed through facial expression. The grasshoppers disgust him. Some fisherman.

My stringer is heavy with fish. You have to keep checking them or the turtles will sneak up on you and eat your fish. My cousin's stringer is empty. He looks up at the sky and makes an ungodly sound. It is almost time to leave. We will have to clean these fish. We will have to bury the fish heads and the fish guts in the garden. The women will be waiting to fry the fish in lard and flour. My cousin makes the Indian sign for grasshopper.

Fingers jump.

I put one on his hook. He smiles.

His bobber makes that desperate plunge that pits you against the struggles of the universe.

Pull.

He immediately catches a walleye. It is a very big fish. Almost big enough to pull the boy into the lake. His fish flops around in the belly of the boat. We pull up our anchor which is a paint can filled with concrete. I row back to shore. Shore with its log cabins and kids and kingdoms of the worms. My cousin does not make the Indian sign for thanks. I receive no thanks for helping him catch a big fish. Bigger than any of my fish. My cousin makes the Indian sign for feast as we near the shore. First you make the sign for work. Then you make the sign for eat, twice. He stands in the boat and holds up his fish. A prize of some enormity.

There is no silence in his vision now. All the men will have to tell the story of that day they caught one just like it. The women will shake their heads, saying nothing as women are apt to do. My cousin leaps from the boat and pulls us onto the shore. Shore where the women and the men regard these raggedy fishermen with awe. Home with food. Tomorrow it will be worms. His were the singing secrets of the lake where light slants down and the only sound the blackbirds make is the rushing of wings. His was the silence of the lake and the absence of his pain. His was the silence of the lake and the wind kicks up clouds that will bring us rain.

# 18

# Invisibility

MOSE ZAH lives in a hogan south of Coyote Canyon near Nazhoni. The area is remote, not quite the desert but a world unto itself. Most of the Indians who live here are invisible, which doesn't mean they cannot be seen. They are mostly seen through, and rendered ethereal. It's the kind of place where you might assume nothing lives, nothing could live, but of course you would be wrong. Indian grass lives here, rabbit brush lives here, gopher snakes live here, sparrow hawks live here, and so do horses.

The Chuska Mountains are to the west and the Chuska Valley is to the north. According to the Navajo map, to get to Mose Zah's place, you cross Coyote Wash for about half an hour going west out of Standing Rock. Turn left on the old dirt road with the wire fence. Go south toward Twin Lakes. Turn right where there are two old trailers and an outhouse. Follow that road up to where that old grandma keeps her sheep and goats. You will see a small hogan near a ridge built between two red rocks. Mose Zah lives there.

The small corral will be ungated and empty.

I first met Mose at the rodeo in Nahadishgish. He was riding bulls. I was writing about riding bulls. I was of the opinion, an opinion that has not changed, that you have to be a little crazed to want to tangle with those hooves and horns.

Mose was very good at being able to stay on the bull for at least thirty seconds before the bull bucked him off. Thirty seconds is a lifetime. Mose Zah offered to show me how to ride the bulls but I declined (which amused him and all the other rodeo cowboys enormously). You couldn't know Mose without knowing someone who was filled to the brim with the vigor of his cowboy life.

White people think of the reservation as a place of rodeos and powwows, and to a certain extent they are right to think this. But the reservation is a lot of other things, too.

In order to know the reservation you have to look past the merely visible and you have to begin to see things that do not so obviously present themselves.

White people don't think of the reservation as a place of AIDS because such notions don't neatly fit the stereotypes. We don't think of the reservation as a place of AIDS because we (even those of us who have lived here) cannot know the reservation. It's too big and has too many mysteries. Yet the harsh realities that plague that other so-called civilized world plague life here too. Sometimes in spades.

AIDS is not a gay disease, and it isn't limited to people who shoot drugs, either.

I have known many heterosexual men who have taken comfort in the stereotypes that are presented to them by a white media determined to put everyone and everything into one box or another. It is a mistake. They are at risk sometimes, too.

AIDS is hardly confined to the limits of a city. AIDS is hardly confined to the limits of a sexuality. AIDS is not confined to racial minorities who shoot drugs (which most Indians cannot afford). AIDS is not confined to the neat definitions the mainstream media would have us believe. AIDS is not confined because the various definitions we use to construct a picture of who we are as a people are not always so cut and dried. Who will and who will not get AIDS is not always black and white. Today AIDS is a part of every reservation in America. Indians in cities live with AIDS, too.

Indians on the reservation with AIDS are truly the invisible among the otherwise invisible, and there are Indians who would even deny that they exist.

Mose and I have never discussed how he got AIDS. It's just not a subject open for discussion. I do not know if he is gay. I do not care.

It's one of those private places most men do not go.

It's too intimate. What is, is.

My knowing how Mose Zah got AIDS wouldn't make him better.

"They said it was AIDS," he told me after a hospital visit in White People Town. It was one of those moments in life when you're wondering *why pick me?* But they did pick you (you wish they hadn't), and there it is. He swallowed hard after he said it. We were sitting on the top rail of his corral and I remember almost falling off. I wasn't thinking about his courage at the time but it took some courage to tell me. You could only say it once. It wasn't something you could take back. It wasn't a truth you could reconstruct. I was surprised he told me at all. I knew he had been sick. No other explanation was offered and none was asked for. I was either going to be his friend through this or I wasn't. Mose was never complicated. What you saw was what you got.

It's a lot like riding bulls at the rodeo. With any luck you can ride it for a while. You hang on. Your life in your teeth. Avoiding horns and hooves.

When you do hit the ground, you tend to hit it hard.

His was a world of hay, Wranglers, Airstream trailers, sweat, heat, and dust that seemed to cling to the inside of his mouth, strange and sweet and rising from the ground. His was a world of hanging on even as the animals that screamed to scrape him off flung him with their forthright weight into the dirt where he sat briefly stunned and coiled like a spring about to spring again. His was a world of manifest masculinity where the boundaries between women and men sometimes seemed set in stone.

Even small, isolated places have their own versions of the village hero, and here in this place where the rodeo nourishes everything, it's the rodeo boy with his blue jeans, ropes, boots split down the backbone, and bruises who holds the attention of the females who compete to feed him pieces of their sun. His was the world of hurts and grunts and cards and women. There is a picture on the wall of his hogan of Mose with a woman at the rodeo in Tucson. There is another picture on the wall of Mose with a woman at Disneyland. Neither woman is around today. I remember women hanging around the edges of the rodeo. I kept telling him that he should avail himself of the companionship of women who were rodeo participants, but he just looked at me as if I had no idea what I was talking about which I did not. He was never all that discriminating about the women. He always seemed amazed that they wanted him. You hold the light from a woman like you hold a winning hand of aces close to your cautious smile. Something in me thinks the women were a camouflage.

There were always many women in his life, a life lived on the small-town Indian rodeo circuit, and his leather wallet was filled with dollar bills. One week you're in Crownpoint, another week you're in Winnemucca. One week you're in Flagstaff, another week you're in Grants. It was a life he lived as easy as a song, and all the notches on his fence post represented his conquering certain ornery animals who had warned him they would kick him if he dared to ride them, and he did. One hand held high in the air between the shifting gravities halfway to the moon. All his women and all the animals he rode could bounce him abruptly off into a shuddering and a scrambling of his cowboy bones.

His was a world of blankets in the beds of pickups and bits of hay in his socks and hair. His was also a world of seeking momentary comfort with women he really didn't know. His was the neon lure and fix of the carnival, rodeo night life rocking powwow at a hundred different community gyms. His was a world where he was proud to own two pairs of cowboy boots: the dirty ones and the shiny ones. The shiny ones were from Texas.

His was a world warmed by a potbellied stove and the cries of birthing ewes and helping his neighbors shear their sheep for the wool money. His was a world where the silver and turquoise jewelry got displayed on the luminescence of his person at just about every Saturday night rodeo carnival he could strut his way through (wearing his shiny Texas boots) with his chest puffed out like a peacock. All the buckle bunnies who assembled to see this manly show would giggle behind their hands. Showoff. All his real friends were men. His women were accouterments.

He was more than most of them could handle, and he knew it, too, which didn't mean they didn't try. His was a world where someday he would move to Denver, buy a lawn mower so he could mow his grass, knowing in the back of his mind he would never move to Denver. His was a world where his body always sought the solace of the ground, and never did sprout wings or fly away bucked up by an angry Brahma bull into the clouds. His was a world of the new ways, and the old ways are worn rusty from misuse. His was a world where he scoffed at a belief in spells, knowing in the back of his Indian mind that he did indeed believe in spells. His world never lasted longer than the thirty seconds he was usually allowed to hang on to his captive bones before being thrown twisting into the air again.

His was a world where the bulldogger rides by steers on horseback. You jump onto the horns and wrestle the steer down until all four hooves are pointed in the same direction. His was a world where his own invisibility—now even as he thins—grows like the tumors in his throat with their secret destinations you cannot fathom. Thrown up into the air now, his hardened figure, birdlike, jumps onto the horns, horns slashing at his not-thereness like knives whisper past his sleeping face, a male mystique of complex confrontations, victorious like the buzzards, a tangle of boots and dust and big cracks in the superficial exterior. His Indian baptisms are all by fire. His was not a world of profound reflection.

His was a world where invisibility in all its many forms was dead as nails and not a surprise or something unexpected as he rides homeward in the blur of dusk. His was not a primitive mind. Neither was it complicated by entanglements he wrongly thought applied to an urban life. Sexuality is irrelevant.

The reservation is not a place where the nearly invisible can transform themselves opaque — and not have to worry about things like wearing condoms — because the ravages of the earth are far away and do not apply to them. The reality versus the myth of it is that the ravages of the planet apply more to them as the idea of who they are becomes diminished, and invisibility assumes the attributes of time and place. Kicked high in the air, Mose never was invisible until he himself believed in it. Thrown from his animals he always found his face ground back into the dirt of things, the valley of his silences inhabited between the adoration of women who did love him for a minute of his awe, and for his indolence and his jumping onto horns and other places they would never go.

I drove him into White People Town once so he could see his doctor at the Indian hospital, thinking, Oh, good, they're going to keep him. And sitting in the crowded waiting room with the coughing grandmas wrecked by tuberculosis and the children who played and cried all around the floor. Him emerging from some desperate examination, elated he could leave, slipping away by inches, and even here wearing his cowboy hat at a jaunty angle, and knowing himself (but not exactly what happened to him, although he pretends), and the strangers in his life walking straight into his heart.

"I can go home now," he said, his eyes never sipping the medicine of bitterness, not because he was any different from the rest of us but because he did not know how.

Me seeing all the dead warriors buried in the sand. Him living with his illness now like one lives next to some great river where the depth is quiet and you stand ready to lose the world with its weight and volubility.

Me driving him home wondering what goes on inside his head, noting that sometimes his fingers tremble.

The word got around all the gossips about what was wrong with him. People came by less and less as he grew smaller, and what was once simply an echoing isolation became a resounding empty chair and all the ropes had wrapped themselves around his cowboy throat. I wonder why he picked me to be his friend. And then I realize it's because I come to him in fragments like the horses here, seeing beyond the stoic pillars of his tempered invisibility, seeing him toil and fight for his balance, seeing him crouched on the ground, enduring a nobility that never was, avoiding horns and now abandoned, acquiesced to the erasure of indifference.

He could no longer ride in the rodeo but would break like glass and wound himself upon the horns even as his fans stand deliriously cheering at the brawl of man and dirt and animal furiously dislodging their separate selves to limp slowly from the spectacle of the rodeo arena. His invisibility is forever branded with his vast array of scars—drunk and fed—and when the winter comes for which there is no cure he will drag himself across the snow to see the running of the horses.

Cowboys don't get AIDS. Indians don't get AIDS. The reservation is not a place of AIDS. Only gay men who live in cities get AIDS. Only IV drug users get AIDS. And mythology crawls through the shadows, tough, hardly reticent, and rots like fruit sits burning in the sun, and truth inhabits the little seed ideas that never get expressed because to articulate the truth is to howl into some uncertain abyss. The reservation is a place where the ravages come, too.

We do not speak of what became of him. Him dying alone out here with the bumblebees. No more setting course for the next rodeo and wrestling with branded calves. Women and animals yielded to his grip. Women and animals filling their eyes with rage and fire. Him hard into the dirt. Does it matter how this man contracted AIDS beyond the fact he has it? Bending his performances and his nights against the stones, he has no words, no concept really (although it has been explained to him) of what has happened to him, now living out his dreams on antiviral medication.

On the reservation there is an enormous stigma attached to Indians with AIDS. AIDS education came to Indian country late. There are still many who have not gotten the word, and there are many who have gotten the word but don't believe it. There are still many Indian men who couldn't tell you what safe sex is. Such a subject could acutely embarrass them and make them scoff. And even if they knew, they wouldn't want to think about it. Mose Zah used to have many friends. Now he is mostly by himself. He sold his animals at the onset of a painful arthritis and peripheral neuropathy.

He doesn't get around like he used to. He doesn't wear his cowboy boots. Now he wears his moccasins. He doesn't ride bulls at the rodeo. In fact, he doesn't even go to the rodeo. Such a trip would be too exhausting. There are days he is confined to a rented drugstore wheelchair.

He has no phone. There is no way to announce that I am coming to see him.

He used to take me riding (these were riding lessons even if we never called them that). I used to take him fishing (these were fishing lessons even if we never called them that).

"Just come," he says. "You know you're always welcome here."

Sometimes I bring groceries, which I know he'll need, but the real reason I come to see Mose Zah is to take him into the desert wilderness so he can sit in his rented drugstore wheelchair and watch the horses. I am able to lay these riches in his lap. I put the cowboy and the wheelchair into my truck and we take off to where the horses run.

There are no people here.

His stealthy gaze sees into some quiet mystery, impassive, penetrating into places neither he nor I have known before.

There are simply some places men do not go together. To do so is to tempt upheaval. We do not speak of AIDS or what has happened to him, preferring to drive way out here among the ridges and the blue distances where horses run lean against the sky. Just to be here is enough. I know he sees visions of the self that was, even as he lives in the broken shell he is today. Sometimes the horses allow us to watch them from the relative comfort of the truck. More likely, though, I have to push his rented drugstore wheelchair off the road and into the wild. I grit my teeth and do it. The red rocks and the sandy hills are sculpted by the whispered beauty of finality.

I can't give him his life back. But I can give him this.

Seeing horses.

All of us are runaways.

It is at least as good as a Safeway sack of groceries.

Eagles fly here, too, high above the cottonwoods and the cliffs. Eagles offering no apologies in their objection to our intrusive presence.

Me wondering if he will die sometime in the midst of winter before he sees the spring. There is no cure for winter. No warmth to taunt the bony sun. Him sitting in his wheelchair, hands folded, forever bent and twisted at having surveyed his thirty-second rodeo rides and more women than he can count, screaming his outrage at the echoes of the distant hills. Me saying nothing. Let it come like hailstones the size of golf balls pouring down from a black and angry passage whose wings enfold the promise of tomorrow and the howling of today.

And then we hear them dully in the distance. Horses with their colts running toward us in undulating melt. Horses with their fear in their nostrils crashing through the neighbor's corn. Mose's eyes singing some pieces of a song I do not understand. Relieving paralysis, the coming of the horses. The horses run in pounding breathlessness all around both our graves. These holes we dig as men, as friends, as fathers, as sons, as husbands. His riotous thoughts hold electric imaginary reins as if to ride sprays of wind upon the backs of spilling horses, bursting into life with their breath again, the grateful running of the horses, stirring all the prairies of the universe with sacred leaps, and thirty seconds of this stirring is all you ever had because that is all there ever was and that is all there is. Thirty seconds and the color of smoke all around you as you wonder at the awesome running of the horses — flying and falling and biting in a buzz of flies—resonating something carried forward in the urgently escaping terror of the horses, whirlwinds into the specter of his sleep.

The coming of the horses is not unlike a burst of rain from some expected thundercloud arriving overhead. Running like a scar across a wild terrain.

I know the horses bring him many things. Power, a harvest of the horses, he can hear the planets move now, lumbering in a rhythm like the hooves, the pounding of a tribal drum, light dancing on the straining necks of horses, horses carried in the air, breaking chests, swept away to unknown sorrows, the movement of the horses bringing balance to the silence of the desert, driving like his memories will always dance with ponies and his women who have left him here.

I wonder if he was vulnerable before. I do not know but suspect he was. Vulnerability being one of those places men do not lightly entertain. Perhaps he was but I never saw it, preferring to see the toughness of the cowboy, not realizing that this, too, would go. I take him home. He is now beyond exhausted. He points out where his garden used to be, but it's like attempting to shift the rotation of a galaxy of stars, and today the absence of a garden (now clumps of dirt and dust) aligns itself with the landscape of an alien planet. The horses have come and gone and rattled the ground here with the supernatural tremors of their running set ablaze. I take him into his hogan where the silence is a bitter violence wrapped all around his unraveled prayers and my prayers, too.

The rodeo women, with their swaying hips encased tightly in their jeans who once laughed with him in bars and drank whiskey with him and played cards with him and danced their broken wings between his legs, have disappeared. I lift him from the wheelchair and marvel at how he seems to grow lighter every time I do it. He sinks into his bed. Only his hands are heavy. It's not a place most men would ever go—putting another man to bed—but modesty has no shape in the coming of the darkness with its dissolving sway over the crumble he has become. Him sleeping there as if he had been born blind. Me wondering where all his women are now and I am a Tewa cherry bow unstrung but fully bent and cannot make his world or mine any softer than this darkness will permit.

All masculine decorum is mute, no longer an illustration of what lurks beneath the skin but lost from view, this version languishes just under his Navajo blankets on his bed, more and more his mountaintops, not of events, but a place of dreams still tethered to the world. AIDS is a disease of loneliness, too. Sex is irrelevant. Gender only is.

There is no prescription for his loneliness, a symptomatic heaviness having more to do with his eyes than with his weight. He never was sardonic or very skeptical, but found his own unnervingly impossible forms of happiness in the most simple enlivening things: his garden, his new truck, the way the sunset seems to slightly falter, and, of course, his horses, which eventually he had to sell as he found himself faltering, and the world (and the women of the world) no longer found its way to him. How can you help someone who has never needed help, never asked for anything, but even now holds tightly to his pride as you yourself grapple with your reconstructions, reserving judgments because in retrospect they are always wrong.

"Just sit with me for a little while," he manages to say. I have worn him out by coming here. By taking him out to see the horses. Every time I visit there is less and less of him to see. And so you sit there because you didn't realize that taking him out to see the horses would drain what reserves of strength he had managed to save in the hope you would come for him, put him in his rented drugstore wheelchair, and transport him in his early retirement to that infinite place not too far away where the horses run, and then you realize without his having to say a word that this is something he used to do with his women. Take them out to see the horses, showing them the solidity and depth of his experience, and bringing the women back, and making love in the very bed where he now remains curled around all the lavish memories he cannot contain. His bed is not my business. His memories are not my business. It is too close.

I look around his tidy space (even the laundry has been put away) and it occurs to me that he has not eaten anything in some time, and so I paw around the neatness and the cans, feeling awkward, feeling like a woman, until I find some soup. I knew there would be soup. I am not great in a kitchen, the kitchen of another man representing territory strange and foreign. Breaching his masculinity and mine, I sit there at the side of his bed feeding him hot chicken noodle soup, and the simplicity of it does not shame me but surprises me, taking me places on these horses I never knew I would go. One spoonful at a time, and I am careful not to spill hot soup on him. Him dubious about being fed like this yet unable to hold the spoon. Feeding another man (something I have never done or thought to do) is more an act of stealth than an indication of masculine necessity.

All the bulls he rides are phantoms now masquerading as maniacal precursors to a violence he could never really tame, any more than he could tame the beauty of the women he had loved, or the men. It hardly matters. His secrets are his secrets.

"I never taught you how to ride the bulls," he says.

It is his version of a joke reminding me to hold fast to the histories of offerings and smiles. It is finally all any of us has.

It takes a long time to feed him the soup. There are places in the bare rooms of masculinity most men never venture into where we are forever unprotected from the vision of ourselves and there are no simple answers to any of the mysteries. All men must have their secrets.

The food revives him some and he retrieves a cardboard shoebox from beneath the bed. The shoebox is filled with photographs of here and there, but mainly there are two subjects: horses and women. They all have names and stories and tangents, and you realize he remembers every rodeo, every ride, every marginal solace. He gets up to take his pills, and you never saw so many pills lined up like soldiers, and you wonder how he keeps them straight.

"People stopped coming by," he said.

There is no more time here to pretend. Time is a luxury Mose can ill afford. He is consumed (not knowing for a long time that he was even sick) and the only thing that seems to touch him is the running of the horses, and an intake of his breath summons failure like a chill. But he's quite beyond despair and seems to see well past the place where my inertia slips freely from the bit releasing solitary horses outstretched against the sky.

One never thinks of the reservation as being a place where such men live out the slippage and the beating of their lives. The reservation with its cakewalks, its powwows, its historical epiphanies, its symbolic bingeing on the past, and its cannibalized abandoned vehicles engulfed by rust, the colors of the universe enduring as the men who live here harvest an impotence both mocking and sublime. The reservation where the horses run and the men they run among are not unlike versions of the men from other places who feel the pull and spin of the earth. The reservation with its dancing and its drums has never transformed itself into a garden of redemption where what gets planted outside its boundaries can't grow here. It all grows here, too, and the stars invisible from the center of the city shudder in the reservation wind which defies the definition of their distant refuge.

Whole communities of people have to sit at home and calmly die in their wings like blankets before the word gets out that the seasons of the virus could have been prevented had tongues taken root with courage enough to play witness to the real story of the reservation versus fleeting moral glimpses of the just too late. Perhaps the reservation can never be rendered visible. AIDS education came here *late* like a thin menace invented out of reticence, much in the same way education itself came to the reservation like a farewell performance unfurls when the pity and the terror are done with.

"When will you come back?" he asks. Companionship. Nothing more.

"Soon," I say.

I wash the dishes as ghosts dance outside somewhere in the darkness.

I keep thinking about how much the reservation can be this falling backward into the deep end of night and death, or eluding death rehearses all the choices that we make not in flight but in seeing such mysteries as the rhythms of the horses.

You would never think of someone like Mose Zah as having AIDS because his facelessness doesn't come from any of the familiar places we have been told to read like signs. The reservation is finally an aberration filled with canyons and our buried cores where emptiness is but a prophet too barbarous to believe. It's not supposed to happen to men like Mose. Cowboys don't get AIDS. But there it is, hovering with its death mask and flourishing in its convoluted solitude.

He's been sick for a long time now, and it occurs to me that I have known him longer ill than I knew him when he was well and fit. Fit and riding bulls and horses.

Mose sold his Airstream trailer, and the only remnant of it is the patch of raggedy grass it used to sit on, providing shade.

My dog whines as coyotes howl their mutual forecasts at the coming of the moon up over the mountains. I start my vehicle. Turn on the lights. Piercing the darkness like the refracted light from an iron stove — standing nervously in the shadows of the red rocks — are the shining, illuminated eyes of horses.

# 19

# Flying Solo

*T*HE SOFT buzzing sound of small planes drones overhead. It was the kind of spring where you wanted to see the earth from some vast and distant hill. A hill covered with dandelions. A hill where the wind might blow like corn silk feels soft against the skin. We pretended to be tough, tough as spears lodged in the ribs, but it was simply another adolescent act, it wasn't real, and we were not tough at all, but felt we had to act the part in order to survive. It was the kind of spring where all the things that had once conspired to suffocate you now let you fill your lungs with air. It was the kind of spring that spins slowly homeward through the terrible silence of our adolescent bones.

Adults who tried to figure us out soon gave up.

Going to the moon would have been a smoother ride.

It was spring, and Bad Nell, Frankie Descheene, and I were fifteen. Fifteen and freaks of nature. Nothing had ever been invented that was more weird than the three of us. Frankie and I were awkward, gawky. We thought our ruffian image might disguise us but it never did. It just made authority look at us all that much harder. We were like huge birds that flap and squawk about. At least Bad Nell had tits and this could define her as a woman. She could lead us around (there were no rings in our noses) with her bracelets and her magical amulets.

She knew the tarot cards, too. We were freaks.

We did not fit in with the nice children. Children who lived in nice houses, had telephones in their rooms, cars in their garages, got good grades on their report cards, took the SAT, and at some point could sit back and let the world come to them.

No one we knew took us seriously. No one believed the things that had been done to us. We were a parenthesis of some yet unseen direction and not unlike the dandelions we sat among.

We could sit anywhere until twilight. Even in the snow.

Adults would ask us where we had been and what we'd been doing. We would attempt to answer this—losing ourselves in the crevice of our words—until whatever adult had inquired as to our whereabouts simply shook his head and walked away. We were a place that lived within.

Adults could not have been more baffled than we were with our demon misfit selves. Onerous with such self-assured cutthroat gristle.

Our communication skills were negligible except as they got expressed among us three and we were forgiving.

We didn't stumble all over our words and our feet when it was just the three of us. We were the demon misfits born near the boxcar tracks. We were hypnotized with hunger, with the emptiness itself, and weary as the outer members of the herd that finally turn around to face the other way, gazing with our thirst into the eyes of growling wolves. Creatures of the ditch bitches. We had not been born so much as spit out like the defiance we still wore as afterbirth. Somehow we always managed to find the edges of the herd. We were the stragglers. It would not have been possible for a nice white person to have been our friend. I'm not sure that having grown up makes it much different.

We weren't like anyone we knew.

We didn't talk like anyone we knew.

We didn't dress like anyone we knew.

We didn't want the things other children wanted. Mainly what we wanted was to be left alone.

One of the things that made us different from other children we knew was our belief that there were things alive that spoke to us and didn't seem to speak to them. It is, of course, heresy to believe that things like lakes and rocks and trees could speak to you, or that these things were animate, had inner lives, and were self-aware. But there it was. We believed. We did not know where our belief that such things as fences could sing had originated, but we felt as though we ourselves had already gone extinct. We believed in Spirit People, too, and if we could only touch their essence it would save us, and it probably did.

It was spring, and yet we still wore black because we had invented wearing black, and we could ill afford the delirious brilliance of other clothes.

We came from families that often washed the laundry in a tub by hand.

On your knees with the dish soap.

We knew that most white children did not wash their laundry in a tub or hang it outside on a line to dry.

In many ways (ways that did not always succeed) we were taught to see the world through Anglo eyes, and any resistance to the dominant perspective always gets summarily punished with the accouterment of failure: you flunk out, you are forced out, you are discounted and thrown away, you are beaten, shamed, humiliated in class, and finally graduated illiterate into a society that bases your very value on your ability to interpret the compulsory symbols.

What dreams we had were dreamt amid the wreckage and the rocks. All three of us had been from one end of the country to the other—we knew where all the rest areas were—and so we thought we knew the world. Our arrogance was superficial as we were not imbued with a lifting hopefulness, the magic chambers of other children. Our confidence was like gasoline, and all the synthesis in our heads had ruptured with the tidings of the tyrants. We lived in all the harder places of the bedrock. Our wing bones were unformed.

I wanted to become a writer. I never wanted to do anything else. This desire was the epitome of perversity, because reading and writing were such tortures for me. In this respect nothing has changed. To this day writing words is the one thing that pushes me right over the edge of the cliff. You either fall or fly. I have crashed and burned more times than I can count.

I am very clear about why I wanted to become a writer. It had nothing to do with Ernest Hemingway. I wanted to become a writer because everyone I knew who supposedly knew a thing or two about it claimed it could not be done.

I was fifteen and determined to scale the impossible.

Bad Nell wanted to be a movie star. And she'd look at Frankie and me to agree that her becoming a movie star was nothing more than the essence of sanity given her talent and her looks.

She could cover the scars on her face with heavy makeup.

Frankie wanted nothing more than to fly. Really fly. In airplanes. His nightmare was that he would find his life someday confined to the boundaries of a factory.

"I'll probably be a factory rat if I'm lucky," he said.

We were of the opinion that it was the world itself that sucked, and no amount of explanation could really shed light on the reality that the world we three happened to inhabit was a place of extraordinary violence. Usually a violence directed toward us, although we did not always know why. None of us attempted to make sense of the violence, as all three of us had given up seeking such answers years ago. In that respect we were already old. In other respects we lived at some infantile level. We had decided that the only way to deal with things like black eyes was to put ice on the eye as soon as you can. We did not believe that black eyes could be prevented. We had all been ripped apart at the hinges many times. We knew that the adults who tormented us stood firmly on ancient feudal privileges.

Bad Nell and I sat back on the airport grass and, looking up, watched Frankie fly the rented Cessna. It was spring, and for the one whole hour a week that Frankie flew no black dogs came tearing after us. Bad Nell and I waved at the plane but couldn't really see if Frankie waved back at us. He seemed to soar in a great stream of the universe — the small and flashing drone of a plane — whispering like a spitfire through the thunderclouds above us.

We brought Frankie to the airport on Tuesday afternoons so he could take flying lessons. It seemed that we had been bringing Frankie here forever. Bad Nell and I never went up in the Cessna with Frankie and his flight instructor. We were not intrigued by flying and we thought it might make us throw up, so Bad Nell and I stayed below. Rooted to the solidity of our many failures, we often wondered where Frankie found the fortitude to transform himself into a thing of flight.

"I still can't quite believe he does this," Bad Nell said. "He doesn't even have his driver's license yet."

"Neither do you but you drive anyway," I noted.

Bad Nell just shrugged. "My mom doesn't really care. Unless I wreck the car. But do you know what Frankie's parents would do to him if they found out he was spending all his money on flying lessons?" She made a threatening gesture with her fist.

I had some idea what they would do, but you had to know Frankie to understand the passion he had developed for flying. All the money he earned during the week bagging groceries went into the flying lessons.

But his family couldn't know. And we had to keep our mouths shut. Or Frankie's father would surely beat him to within an inch of Frankie's life. All three of our lives were spent in escapades designed to avoid the belt.

Fifteen is a little old to still be beaten, but we were not big children and had learned to live by our wits, which weren't all that big either.

And the pit we could be pushed into was very deep.

The small flying service (one Cessna) that called itself a school was housed in an old Quonset hut at the west end of the mainly deserted airport. Frankie's biggest problem was getting there. We cut school. Bad Nell drove her mother's car. It was a big old boat of a car that rumbled noisily and clanked like a jackhammer everywhere we went. It was only a matter of time, of course, before we got caught cutting class to come out to the wide open space of the airport so Frankie Descheene might take flying lessons. But until we got caught, we would continue bringing Frankie to the airport on Tuesday afternoons where he would spend one hour in the sky with his instructor, who had been given written permission by Frankie's parents (this note having been entirely devised by Bad Nell) allowing Frankie Descheene to fly his heart out.

Bad Nell signed a few notes for me, too.

In some ways she was like our mother.

The flying lessons were not connected to any school-based academic curriculum, and if they had been, Frankie Descheene would not have been allowed to participate. We were not exactly the kind of students you would have associated with flying lessons.

Or lessons of any sort with one eye on the future.

All it took was cash, and getting there, and one poorly written note.


We were known as the bad kids of the school. The soldiers of our many mutinies marching on. Even the good kids would visibly wince when we got called on in class. It was a mistake to ask us to read aloud, and most teachers only made that mistake once. Our stumbling around the words and attempting to follow lines with our squinting and our fingers were painful to everyone involved.

We sounded out words as if we were chewing gunpowder.

We lived in that vacuum contradictions make. I needed glasses badly.

The fact that I was considered to be slow and stupid did not deter me from reading everything I could get my hands on.

Sometimes I had to read things five, six, seven times before I could understand whatever it was I was attempting to read. My biggest secret was that I loved libraries and could have lived in one, but since I hung out with kids who had a surly attitude I had to have something of a surly attitude, too. My love for books was not unknown to Frankie and Bad Nell. For my birthday they gave me a copy of *The Sun Also Rises* they had stolen from the public library. I never told them that eventually I returned the book.

I hated white people, and the fact that I was one, slurred and mixed, did not prevent me from hating them. White people had hurt me time and time again. I hated white people because I could not understand what it was they wanted, and found that a big, big part of life consisted of giving white people what they wanted. I hated white people, and the fact that hating white people was not going to help me understand them in the least did not dissuade me from hating them at all. I wanted to become a writer because it was the only form of revenge I would ever have. Not realizing that writing is also a holding together of the fragments and the pieces. The writers I read all seemed to construct little mechanisms of vengeance here and there. I wanted some of that, too. I screamed to make some sense of my life.

I wanted to be James Baldwin. His books were not allowed in our school library. I didn't understand that people like James Baldwin had enemies too, real enemies, people who hated him for what he thought and wrote. And then, of course, there was the color of his skin. I wanted to be James Baldwin because his books had been banned by our schools, and I could not think of anything more delicious than to be banned.

Not realizing I had banned myself from most of the good things (like football) that went on in White People Town.

I liked the flow that words could make and found you could escape in the current of that river. You did encounter rocks and obstacles but at fifteen I had yet to fathom that rocks and obstacles could be dangerous. I wanted to create worlds like the worlds found in Indian myths, and I wanted to kidnap white people into this world and not let them out. Bad Nell and Frankie hated white people, too. We three would bitch about white people while we did our laundry in the bathroom tub.

The nice kids with the nice homes and nice clothes didn't like us much. No college or university was looking to accept us or looming on the horizon of our years. Our academic achievements were few and far between.

I was a white-looking racial slur of mixed mongrelism that even the white students could not quite define. Bad Nell was Indian and black. Frankie was Indian and Mexican. Where I was a mystery, Frankie and Bad Nell were more definitely constructed. Frankie had worked the fields as a migrant worker. What money there was in the Descheene family did not go into such nonsense as flying lessons.

We were a threesome and we flaunted it. Not that any of it was ever sexual. We were all so shy we hardly ever took our clothes off even when we were alone. If we went swimming in the gravel pits — this was strictly forbidden, as Mexican bodies were always being pulled out of there, blue as new denim — we kept our clothes on. Our relationship wasn't sexual but we didn't let the world know that. It amused us to let the world think it was indeed that kind of threesome, or maybe it might be, and while boys believed it, and were easily scandalized, girls never believed it and treated us like annoying insects.

"We're vermin," Bad Nell would say.

For our part, we liked the initial impact of appearances, and we went out of our way to leave the impression that it could have been sexual, not realizing that what we were was simply odd and strange. Players at the freak show.

We took pains to be suggestive.

Three very, very out-of-place fifteen-year-olds dancing the dirty dance together at high school dances in their knee-high moccasins with the flying fringe.

Of course, we never told anyone we had seen more real dancing than this at any number of the powwows we had attended.

Our suggested sexuality was nothing more than an empty room at dusk. Three juveniles dancing and snapping snakes and mounting chaos from behind like a tomcat and worshiping the dragon's breath. Not one person in the world approved of us, and all the nice white jocks suspected that we were the perverts who had stolen their jockstraps as if to rob these boys of their rightful potency.

Bad Nell had a real talent for breaking into lockers. "Piece of cake," she'd say.

Highway robbery was just a fact of life.

Bad Nell could tell who owned what jockstrap just by sniffing it. "White boys have a very distinct smell to them," she claimed, nostrils flared. We'd laugh.

If you really want to draw blood from some nice white boy, steal his jock as if it were a totem.

The nice white kids gave us plenty of room. Being ostracized was what we hated more than anything, yet being ostracized was what we seemed to cultivate. One is only fifteen once.

We three had a difficult if embracing camaraderie as we walked down the hall to class. The adults would glare. What we had was a loyalty that submitted to an instinct that defied the vertigo of normal friendships. Normal anything was viewed by us as at least suspicious, at best about as enduring as an anecdote, or just another thing that turns sourly into a grievance, and we already had enough of those.

"Ever notice how white people are shocked at their own racism?" Bad Nell would say. "But Indians know and just say 'hmmm.'" Racism was ordinary.

"Hmmm," I said, hoping that this would make me sound more Indian than I was.

Frankie's dad did not speak English. "His dad will beat him," Bad Nell said. Watching Frankie fly.

Frankie had his flying lessons.

I had my many notebooks. Stupid or not, I was always writing furiously in my notebooks. Wild metaphorical parallels delivering in full swing my enemies to pits and bargain basements of their own and sending these two friends I have—and I am lucky to have them—into laughing fits of sheer literary hysteria when they read the words I have put together like strings in the wilderness. The wilderness is never truly tame. I am set ablaze with words but keep my silence, too, gripped by a nervous vigilance that guards against complete collapse and terror with its ability to sexually swallow you even as you shrivel. My words were knives that lived in the eyes, driving through my sated heart, shaping something solid from the shatter, farewells, passionate designs, and things half done I had seen along the roads that had led me here.

Bad Nell had her red lipstick, her cigarettes, her chewing gum, and her mother's car.

Bad Nell had her grandmother, too. Bad Nell's grandmother lived on a reservation, and Bad Nell would escape there when things got really bad at home.

Bad Nell's grandmother was an Anishinabeg.

. . .

What we three had in common beyond our failures was the fact that we could be beaten, had been beaten, and probably would be beaten again. Physically beaten for transgressions we did not always understand.

The three of us were of the solid opinion that the nice white children from nice white families were never beaten—they'd been given everything. But what did we know? We were fifteen.

It was not an accident that we found one another.

"I'll take you up in the plane after I'm certified," Frankie tells us.

Bad Nell and I say nothing. We will have to call upon our courage.

At fifteen we were completely unreachable and lived in an inspirational trance of our own making, hopeful only in the sophomoric belief that when we became adults (if we lived that long) it would get better. As adults no one would abuse us. We did not know that the boxcar borderland we lived in was an amorphous thing and could travel with us to the end of our self-defeating days like a telepathic hallucination. Maps might tell us where we were, and we could grow proficient at reading them, but only supernatural exorcism of a kind we had yet to fathom could lure us from our monolithic trance. We were the demon misfits born near the boxcar tracks, a place of weathered light and somber hues and a sullenness that clung to our mouths, our eyes, our clothes, and we knew (because we had been told) our inner music might be fierce, but it was no match for the hunger and the cold and the ditch and the rags you wore and the city buses—always buses, disgorging their noise and their soot on you—that never, ever went as far as the airport.

It was the burning symbolism of the place, a place where one of us with help from the other two could temporarily flee, be really gone, pushing out, and the engine of their white indifference didn't matter here, here where you went round and round (becoming lost once) in circles far above it all. We knew what made Frankie fly even if all the world conspired against it.

Seeing Frankie fly was our one victory over the vacuum that defined our lives.

Bad Nell kept the jockstraps she stole (and the ones she made Frankie and me steal for her) in a shoebox she had stashed in the bottom of her hallway locker. The locker smelled. But she wanted a piece of them anyway, knowing that something of theirs, something private, was hers.

Even in our hardest, most cynical times, there was something crystalline inside the armored furnace we carried around, and even with its flaws we would sometimes remove it from the pressures that sustained it, and we would marvel like three feral cats that we were alive at all. We would hold that secret up among ourselves — improbable as it was — and know that even exile could be ignited with the little holes we burned through things like sky.

That was why Frankie flew, and that was why, even on the ground for one whole hour a week, we, too, flew with him and escaped the worn-out ashes and the coughing blood despair of the world we lived in. We may have been demon misfits, judged by the nice white children we knew to penance, but we had been assembled with an advancing toughness that would steal their socks and their jockstraps and their new September-school-sale gym shoes. We were driven by a muse they would never know, never dance to kicking, and the fact that none of them would do this, none of them would come out here to learn to fly, only made us more determined, more steadfast in our belief that if we did not do this we would implode.

The school we went to (between the three of us we had attended over a dozen different schools) did not crank out pilots,
writers, and movie stars. The school we went to cranked out
white, cookie-cutter versions of factory-rat success. Some kids
did go on to college, but you had to have someone there who
said *do this*, and not many of us stragglers in the herd had that.

We three missed a lot of school on Tuesday afternoons. We had
not prepared for the day it would catch up with us. Apparently
there were phone calls between the school and our homes.

I am greeted at the door with the swinging of the belt. I am
left bewildered by this contempt and know better than to say
anything about airports and flying lessons. And the blackness
lifts me out unrepaired and wet with blood which must soak his
belt, and I cannot fathom how he wears these stains of me
around his waist like a badge of masculinity finds its sacredness
transfixed in the blur of these stupefied performances. I am all
his hated rail yards, factories where he has worked to put food
on the table, fields he has picked, rows and rows, and all the
blackened soot he has ever breathed. I am yet one more menial
task to him. Someone who never did earn his keep. My eyes are
closed and there is no vanishing point at which all the sweat
and whipping me must stop. Each small act of my defiance a
false claim against him and one more reason to whip my back
as if strolling through the asylum grounds. I did prefer his belt
to his touching me, though. I am a sack of tendons tossed about
and sewn together where the small bones heal and the eyelid
turns from black to yellow back to whatever color it should be
again. And it's the memory that gets mopped up even while
something awakened and absolute inside the pieces and the
fragments undergoes diminishment like an echo sings farewell.
Their parents are waiting for Bad Nell and Frankie De-

scheene, too. We would lick one another's wounds like dogs at a private annihilation. This place where you sink to shadows mute with the sonic weight of center stage.

All my notebooks are thrown into the trash.

I would rather that he touch me than throw my notebooks into the trash. Punishment.

It was the kind of spring where you wanted to see the earth from some vast and inaudible paralysis.

I wouldn't be an adolescent again for all the money in the world. Who would want to go through that? But I go back to Frankie and Bad Nell's place (now that their children are grown and gone) because we are somehow always fifteen again and foolish.

Bad Nell and Frankie live together in a rundown house one block from the rundown house Bad Nell had lived in as an adolescent. Frankie has worked in an automobile factory for over twenty years. Bad Nell is a sometime waitress and still hypnotizes all the men with her bracelets and her magical amulets.

They scream and howl when I ask Bad Nell what she did with all those jockstraps. She does not remember. What we remember is a selective thing and what the three of us remember is the airport.

They ask if I still write everything down in notebooks. My finished manuscripts are burden enough, so I don't keep notes on anything. We three talk about the writing life although Frankie and Bad Nell have never lived it.

I explain how the tenaciousness I was always advised to hang tight to finally led to homelessness and nothing more. "Writing and publishing is perhaps more of a white people game than even we gave it credit for way back when," I said. "I look white to you and to everyone else but for the life of me I still do not understand what it is white people want. I can't figure out the conventions, and when I do it's like a noose around my neck. I look white to you, but the people I write about aren't white and so what I do gets assigned to that niche where we're all familiar with the edges. The literary world is very, very white. It's left me savoring my bitterness over twenty years of complete failure."

The three of us go back in time in the flashing of an instant. Perhaps we are always really there.

"Do you hate writing now?" Bad Nell asked. She always went for the bone.

"I do," I said. I said it softly for it was the truth. I had nothing to show for it. Not even a collection of notebooks. All I had was a dog and some maps in my truck that went everywhere.

To hate something deeply that you once loved is the final triumph of the vacuum. It's like being touched by your dad but in the bad ways.

"You know, I pour coffee all day and my feet ache," Bad Nell said. "But I don't hate what I do because I have Frankie." Companionship.

She never went to Hollywood. She never challenged the authority of the images. But she did one big goddamn thing. She had children and she was kind.

She hugged Frankie closer to her on the couch. Going to these places where other people never go is what we were about. In that respect nothing had changed.

"I was asked to come to this literary event, a reading where real writers would read from things they had published, and they wanted me to read an article I had written about my dead son," I said. "So I'm standing there reading this *thing* and I can't see it anymore because the paper and the print are soaked and smeared. I didn't realize I had been crying. And now other places want me to appear and read from the same article like licking and licking an open wound and I can't. I can't do it. I put it away in this really safe place and I can't open it all back up again. I tell them I'll read something else but no. They want what they want and that's it. I don't know how to give white people what they want anymore and it has just about destroyed me."

The things I thought were important were not important.

The things I did not think were important were important.

It did not matter what I wrote about. None of it could get published.

I explained how I had written an entire novel about Indians and how it had been returned to me by an editor ripped into little pieces.

Frankie says, "Hmmm."

I had failed at writing fiction. I had failed at telling the story of the Navajo. If anything is onerous, it is grief.

Among the three of us Bad Nell had always been the one who could take the stuff Frankie and I brooded over and toss it into the air. Like confetti.

This is why she had been a great broad at age fifteen. This is why she was a great broad now.

"When I used to believe that stuff, too, you know, when they used to say I was the school screw-up, that's when I'd steal their damn jockstraps," Bad Nell said. "Remember when the alert went out for the jockstrap thief? That was me."

We laughed again. We knew.

We had even helped her steal a few.

"I never laid a hand on my kids," Frankie said. One claims victory when one can. Personally, I thought Frankie should proclaim it from the rooftops.

"My kids like me. In all those years I never hit them because I remembered what we went through, you know, being whipped and knocked around." Heroism comes in many quiet forms. Like being touched but in the right ways.

Sometimes it's about what you don't do.

There are smiles of revenge all around and Bad Nell runs her fingers through Frankie's hair. She had always loved him far more than me. As for me, I was in love with what they had. "Frankie was a real good dad," she says.

We look at photo albums. There are no pictures of my Tommy. I have no walls to hang them on. Someone took a picture of the three of us dancing in our moccasins with the knee-high flying fringe. There are several pictures of small planes parked at airports.

Frankie finally got his pilot's license but he doesn't fly much anymore.

We three drive to the airport anyway. It's all new now and there's a terminal there that accommodates the big jets. Today the bus goes all the way.

No one beats us anymore. It was a pit invisible to strangers where time slowed and we were emptied of everything.

There were the beatings that produced visible bruises. Then there were beatings of another kind. The beatings of diminishment. One form is bad enough. Combine the two and you have done a terrible thing to a person. You have raped him.

Bad Nell still has the scars on her face. People just call her Nell now. She did not become a movie star but settled for her life as a waitress and a mom. "We survived those times," she tells me. "I think it was something of an accomplishment." Sometimes I am not so sure. The music from the belt still rips me from the hinges. The music from his touch still sings and singes. Now that I am not fifteen I know we were never made from bronze.

Or onerous gristle.

But we had been assembled as some antitheses to the vacuum.

The soft buzzing sound of small planes drones overhead. It was the kind of spring where you wanted to see the earth from some vast and wise perspective. All the things that had once conspired to suffocate us now let us fill our lungs with air.

Bad Nell and I sit in a parking lot watching Frankie flying solo.

Anyone who thinks that clouds don't speak is crazy.

# 20

# My New Wife
# Is a Teacher

*A*FTER FAILING at just about all of my relationships in life I decide that I have to be hopeful even in the face of contradicting evidence. There is a part of me that refuses to give up hope, that says I am capable of connecting to another human being. I quietly refuse to give up trying.

Writing has taught me one damn thing. How to be tenacious.

In the past I blamed many of my failures on the fact that I'm a writer and it's damn difficult to live with one. For one thing, there's no money in it, and if you do hook up with a writer don't expect to participate in many of the rituals of life. I have always blamed my profession for my failures when in fact the failures rest with me. I decide to be hopeful anyway.

My new wife is a white woman who works as a teacher at the Bureau of Indian Affairs school just down the dirt road from where I lived on the Navajo Nation.

In the past I could always hide behind my half-breedness, my slur of racial mongrelisms, the ditch I was born in. I am not entirely white, only part everything. I could hide behind my many camouflages like a dog on the loose in White People Town. But not this time.

My life is rich beyond measure because my wife comes home with stories. Stories about the children she teaches.

Curiously enough, she has some half-breeds in her classroom.

I think that most teachers go into the classroom with a fair amount of balance, but I don't know how you come away from it without favorites. There are kids you don't like all that much. There are kids you tolerate. And then there are kids who make your day. You develop favorites.

My wife's kids are in the first grade. Some of these kids are like shadows. These are the kids who never miss a day of school. They stay late to help clean the blackboards. They pound the chalk from the erasers. They do little shadow things quietly the way a shadow sneaks up on you although you knew it was there all the time. It elongates as the day wears on. It becomes a part of you.

Sometimes the shadows come home with you in the form of stories. Sometimes the shadows come home to you in flesh and blood.

I had heard about Mosika. He was a dark Indian boy who

rode his bike around and around the parking lot of the Indian school. Turns out he's a half-breed—part Navajo, part Mexican. My wife tells me he spends most of the day under his desk or under a table in the classroom. I ask her if she tolerates this. She says she does.

"I need to be able to give him time to deal with the increased demands of school," she explained. "In time, he'll come around."

I know I did, too.

Every Navajo I have ever met has horror stories about the Indian schools. Stories about how they cut off your hair and dipped you in sheep dip to get the fleas out. Stories about how every shred of dignity you might have had was stripped from you by the people who ran the BIA schools. Stories about how they beat you if you so much as spoke Navajo or Apache or Tewa or Paiute or Sioux or whatever your tribal language was. English was the only language that was tolerated.

A lot has changed at the Indian schools. Today Indian culture is a part of the emphasis put on education within the context of the tribe. No one is punished for speaking Indian. Now the languages sing and dance. The old days may be gone forever but they had a tremendous impact. Something of them lingers like an aftertaste. It would be rare for you to hear Navajo spoken in a Navajo school. The culture that is imitated is usually the culture of MTV. The old days are gone but their legacy remains. Like the legacy of rape.

If you really want to devastate a culture, take away its language.

Take away its stories.

Render its history irrelevant.

It will rot soon like a carcass in the sun. No one will believe it was beautiful.

My wife invites Mosika to dinner. I make barbecue in the backyard. He has never had barbecue before. He wolfs it down like a hungry child. His parents live up the dirt road and they are very poor.

A lot has changed at the Indian schools. But it's too late. Instead of seeking ways to make its schools better, the Bureau of Indian Affairs is getting out of the education business altogether. It has abandoned hundreds of schools in the past few years, leaving them to be run by local communities that have not a shred of experience running a school, or running anything. The BIA has in essence packed up and left.

Like a horse runs away, never to be seen again.

Leave the Navajo for the Navajo.

Now it was happening at the school down the dirt road from where I lived. We were not immune from what white people called downsizing. How do you downsize something that never did have much of a chance to make it in the first place? The BIA has abandoned its responsibilities to the tribes and to the children of the tribes.

We are faced with leaving the reservation. I *hate* the BIA.

I knew it was coming. But I wasn't ready to leave just yet. I was only beginning to know Mosika. He joined me for walks across the Navajo mesa when I had to save my sanity and leave my writing and do something physical like walk the dog. Companionship.

Mosika never said much on our walks across the Navajo mesa, which is a vast place of space and loneliness and many Navajo paths.

And horses, too, that Mosika claims will bite. He is afraid of them as he is a little guy.

· · ·

Eventually Mosika was able to leave the safe confines under the desk or under the table in his classroom. In time he simply emerged, and he learned how to read and write. Sometimes his eyes had that blank look kids with fetal alcohol syndrome get, but he could replace it quickly with something else that veritably sparkled.

We would see the Navajo police cars parked up at Mosika's. The mom would call the cops on the dad. Back to under the desk for a while. But every time he emerged from under his desk, he would stay out for longer and longer periods until he wasn't hiding anywhere toward the end of the school year.

It was time to pack Old Big Wanda. There was no more job at the Indian school and it was time to go. My wife had received other offers and we were going to take one of them. We don't have many things so it's not too hard to pack Wanda with our stuff. Mosika came over and offered to help, but I didn't need help because I did not want him to see me cry. I had been here a long time and I was leaving now. It was a place of many memories. I was going back to the world of white people with vast amounts of visceral apprehension. White people make me nervous.

Mosika helped me pack anyway. You never really need the help of the children who volunteer to help you after school. Until you realize you need them like you need water and air to drink and breathe. Mosika never really believed we were leaving. He could not imagine it. For the first time I began to understand something of the context the reservation surrounds you in. All he knew was the reservation. Anything outside it was a total abstraction.

We're leaving now. Don't forget the dog. I've been bracing myself for this moment. I tell myself I will not look back. I believe it, too. But it is an illusion. The truck moves more slowly with our stuff. I look in the rearview mirror and he's there, of course. Riding his bike around and around what used to be a BIA school for the Navajo. I hold my wife to me tightly.

The reservation runs like blood through a river of my dreams.